The Joining

Blessings –
Vishara

Peace, Light and Joy.
Joanne

The Joining

Vishara Veda

To order additional copies of this book, contact:

Xlibris Corporation

1-888-795-4274

www.Xlibris.com

Orders@Xlibris.com

65874

Contents

Acknowledgements

From my heart I want to extend gratitude to all my spiritual family whose support contributed to bringing *"The Joining"* into print.

First, to Joanne Atwood who has been the anchor that has allowed the writing process to move forward and who recognized the importance of getting this story into the hands of those who are ready for its message. To the women's group who read, critiqued and edited *"The Joining"*, lending their insights and energy to the project: Irene Stewart, Nadya King, Patricia Rice, Jewel Shield, Tula Kyle, Bettie Wood, Denise Patton and, my amazing Mom, Ingrid. To Ted Cutler, a gifted videographer, for always seeing the purity and clear frequency behind *"The Joining"*.

To Anakha Coman who embodies the Divine Feminine; you inspire me with your wisdom and courage.

To my dearest friends, Judith Michaels and Bobbi DePorter; we have walked together for many years and many lifetimes. To Alex and Shannon, you have taught me to "Let Go and Let God" and brought me great joy.

To my Spiritual Partner, Qua, with whom I am blessed to share this adventure in a human body. Only the Divine Plan could have created the life we have together.

Most important, to our other-dimensional Councils and our own Divine Spirit who direct us moment by moment on the path toward service to the Awakening.

Author's Note

"There is another dimension which is our home.
In truth we are not here but there. This is our shadow."
by Rumi

Dear Reader,

Through these pages it is our intent that you embark on a journey through the distortions of the human experience and awaken to your True Identity—that of Spiritual Beings having a very vivid Human Experience. Some of you will find that these stories trigger your memories of other dimensional realities. You will also find opportunities to go beyond your current mental constructs, entering into a world that exists within all of us merely awaiting the opportunity to be awakened. That world is beyond time and outside of the small story each of us created to explain why a specific body type was chosen as our home for this earthly dimension and who we are in this realm.

For many years I experienced an inner calling to write this book and even made a few futile attempts, but the time was not right. The idea just sat percolating inside of me until a few months ago. As the book started to pour through me, I awoke in the middle of the night knowing the time had come. Going through the files in my computer I realized I had written five chapters a few years ago which gave me a concrete starting point.

Early in the process, I contacted my spiritual sister, Joanne Atwood, who is a published author. She agreed to read, critique and edit the book. Soon our journey together became much more intimate; Joanne began living parts of the story—as if she had experienced it along with us. She captured details in several sections that I had not shared with her previously. This is the story of a pre-destined Divine relationship. It is a true story—however some names have been changed and there is an occasional shift in the order of the events for the purpose of creating smooth transitions and clarity for the reader.

Daily life is our training ground. Reading spiritual books, seeking spiritual teachers and gurus, and experiencing mystical practices generate heightened awareness. However, if we, existing as we do in this dimension, do not dedicate ourselves to a larger picture of ourselves and the world, then all the books, teachers and experiences are merely fun, or unusual conversation pieces leading nowhere. If we do not live our lives paying attention to, and embracing, what is right in front of us; if we do not courageously act on a higher calling from within, our past will continue to repeat itself leaving us wondering why the system, the teachings . . . and God, failed us.

Before we see the Light, we must deal with our personal veils in the form of distortional beliefs that reside in the conscious and unconscious mind. It takes courage and a willingness to live in harmony with an inner calling above the illusions of the outer world. There is always more to learn; one thing prepares us for the next.

Spirit is always here, always with us, around us, inside us. May your adventure while reading *The Joining* serve you in your own insights, awareness and spiritual awakening.

Blessings on your journey!

Vishara

Prelude

From the Silence Before Time
The Assignment

"You are that which you seek.
You are a multiple dimensional being
living simultaneously on all dimensions back to the
Oneness.
You created the illusion of separation for the joy of
experiencing a journey back Home to a place
You have only pretended to leave."
~channeled by Zantron~

~ In a parallel reality,
where life is lived in harmony ~

   Multitudes of Light Beings followed Qua Tua' and Vishara along the stone path leading toward a golden temple standing regally on a hill across the valley. In their meditative state, Qua Tua' and Vishara were intensely aware of everything around them. As they moved gently forward, their golden robes brushed the stones of the path; the sound mingling with the chime of bells edging the deep violet sashes flowing downward from the center of each robe.

Adding to the splendor of the procession, and completing the music of the moment, were the sounds from a waterfall flowing over a stone wall, then splashing through tumbling vines heavy with blossoms. Sharing in the rhythm, a soft breeze sighed through the trees, ruffling the feathers of tropical birds while stirring the scents of flowers blooming in breathtaking hues.

———————

Free from the density of lower dimensions, souls played in the curves of unlimited space. Within the physical laws of this reality, all Life Force energy swirls in an unformed mass of iridescent color. Only when one or more fields of consciousness, or Light Beings, focus on a particular form does it manifest out of the particles of light.

In this reality, Beings communicate telepathically using their voices only as a source for chanting, toning and song. All Beings are honored and known to be divine individualized expressions of the Oneness. Thoughts and emotions of doubt, death and fear are not in their awareness, only Love for all in creation and acceptance of each existing moment. To Earthly consciousness, this place would be known as Heaven.

———————

As the first Light Beings accompanying Qua Tua' and Vishara ascended the thirteen stone steps leading to the massive, carved doors of the temple, the message of song was telepathically heard by all. The frequency of their toning joined together signaling the massive doors to swing outward displaying a series of pottery urns overflowing with scented flowers nodding their greeting.

Qua Tua' and Vishara continued to lead the procession through the foyer of the temple toward an open area bathed in golden white light emanating from a bench covered with deep violet satin and trimmed with gold braid. By unspoken agreement Qua Tua' and Vishara approached the center of the room seating themselves upon the bench while the Light Beings of their soul family moved, as one, circling the room.

All were prepared for the communication of the divine assignment. Thousands of angels sang in praise to the joining of the spiritual Truth that unites all creation into the Oneness.

The assembled soul group intuitively acknowledged its surrender into the service of the Higher Good that has no opposite. Only Love . . . IS.

With one fluid motion, Qua Tua' and Vishara stood. In the rhythm of the moment they gently raised their arms to shoulder height, wrists slightly bent and palms up. A golden light began misting upward from their palms in clockwise rotation. These strands of light merged into one, increasing in strength, speed and girth to create a swirling energy that permeating the entire room.

The multiple energies of the gathering vibrated in blissful harmony as they began to create something new that could be described as a separate Being or Group Soul, bringing with it a peace that passed all understanding. This Divine Bliss of unspeakable beauty was maintained until a clear knowing was achieved and all within the soul family understood and accepted the mission of Qua Tua' and Vishara's divine journey.

Lovingly Qua Tua' and Vishara withdrew sufficient energy from the group to surrender back into the illusion of separation. Their assignments were clear. Vishara, along with hundreds of others in her Soul Family were to go, as the first wave, to the reality called Earth in the third dimension. Qua Tua', her other half, was to remain off planet in other dimensional realities.

Vishara accepted the mission to lower her frequency sufficiently and to live in Earth-reality through many lifetimes gathering knowledge, transmuting distortional energies, and supporting evolutionary leaps. Qua Tua' would descend to the third dimension, joining Vishara on their twin soul mission, only when frequencies in Earth's evolutionary journey would allow Divine Relationships to flourish. While waiting, he would watch over evolution as it played out until the conditions were fertile for his first experience inhabiting a human body in support of the liberation from the dream of separation and pain.

In the illusion of time on Earth, the arrival of Qua Tua' was to be many incarnations into the future. In reality, it was happening simultaneously outside of time.

Part One

~ Danielle ~

Chapter One

The End of a Perfect Marriage

"To hear and answer the call to commit
fully to being in my life,
I must learn to be with whatever is,
even when that is a lack of conscious awareness
of the still center."
~Oriah Mountain Dreamer~

~ Many Lifetimes Later ~

With night approaching, the temperature outside was dropping rapidly. The wind howled through the rain slicked streets. I jerked the wheel of my car to miss flying branches and brush as I thought, *"This must be the worst storm the Pacific Northwest has experienced in years."*

As I entered the driveway of my recently rented farmhouse, there was a thunderous crash that seemed to surround me. My body, already tense from the twenty mile drive in the storm, trembled. Looking in the rear view mirror, all I could see were fir filled limbs and branches from a tree blocking the roadway behind me. *"What a perfect metaphor"*, I thought, *"for the paths of my life so recently and permanently closed."*

With my heart drumming in my chest and my stomach churning, I dropped my head on the steering wheel and prayed, "I ask to be released from this fear and disorientation that is dominating my life right now. Allow me to understand my higher truth so that I may be a clear vehicle. I wish from the deepest place to surrender into my True Identity so that its power can be manifested fully. And so it is! Amen."

Taking a deep breath and feeling calmer after praying, I wondered, not for the first time, what had happened to send me away from a wonderful husband and seemingly perfect life. The small community where I served as a minister in a new-thought church was speculating about the same questions. How could I give up a man like Charles? What right did I have to disrupt the lives of my family, my daughters, the church and the community with this separation? Was this just a wrong detour on life's journey that would correct itself with time?

I grieved, fearing it was my own selfish yearnings that had caused the upset in the lives of so many people I loved. I had few answers to the many questions racing around in my head, but I knew I had to go along with what was happening no matter where it would lead me.

Reflecting back, I remembered the day it all started. My daughter, Alex, and I were driving home from her junior high school. Always uniquely conscious, Alex caught me unaware when she said, "Mom, I think we could bring a guy for you into our lives. What if we did a visualization together?"

"Are you thinking you want someone for us?" I replied, somewhat surprised. Alex and I had been a unit ever since my older daughter, Shannon, had gone to live with her father a couple of years before. Alex was very sensitive to the feelings of others and her instinct was always to heal and nurture. I wondered if she thought I was lonely, or, if her strong desire for family was motivating her to want a more traditional unit.

"So, what do you have in mind?"

"Well, I was thinking we could just come up with what we want and tell each other. Then when we get home, when you're not driving the car," she said with a giggle, "We can close our eyes and imagine him coming into our lives."

"Sure, that will be fun. I just hadn't realized that you wanted a guy to join us."

"Well, I've been thinking about it for a while. I know I already have a dad, but lots of the kids at school have step-fathers and maybe you would be happier with someone special. Do you think?"

As always, Alex amazed me with her wisdom and her open heart. "O.K., let's get started." All the way home we described the qualities of our perfect partner and dad. Immediately upon walking into our apartment we sat down for a closed-eye visualization.

Within two weeks, Charles came into our lives. A month later we had moved in together and soon we were engaged to be married. No person I had ever met could have pleased Alex, or me, more.

I had promised Charles, on the day we were married that he was my life partner and that our being together was everything I wanted. Alex was thrilled and Charles, with no children of his own, adored and delighted in both of my, now our, daughters from the beginning.

~The Rose Wedding~

Our marriage had started out like a perfect dream, with a wedding held in a magnificent Tudor mansion on the Malibu cliffs above the Pacific Ocean. It was one of those magically perfect March days gilded with sunlight. The fragrances of newly blossomed flowers filled the air, and birds sang their songs in perfect harmony. Even the peacocks strutted across the lawn displaying their feathers, as if to say that they knew this day would be remembered for years to come.

Joy permeated the very air as the people attending the wedding gathered to share this magical event. They were prominent authors, speakers, seminar leaders, and a smattering of progressive thinking Hollywood types.

Wearing a shimmering beaded gown which caught the light with each step, I slowly moved forward passing the smiling faces of those I loved most in this world. As I floated down the aisle to the piercingly beautiful voice of Amanda McBroom singing her famous song, "The Rose" I felt deeply moved by the words:

"I say love, it is a flower, and you its only seed."

Charles watched me approach with his heart and thoughts visible in his eyes. "This statuesque vibrant woman with her blue-green eyes and thick blond hair is about to become my wife!"

Returning his gaze, I felt a quick flutter at my core. My life had become exactly what I dreamed—that foolish romantic love story of my childhood; to marry, in a fairy tale wedding, a wonderful, strong, kind man who adored me. Together we would build a life, create a home and live happily ever after.

I arrived to stand with my chosen mate and Rev. Marianne Williamson, in a beautiful ceremony, joining us together as husband and wife.

Tears glistened in the eyes of many of our family and friends as Marianne spoke, "God can give you no greater gift than to give you the mission which is beyond the relationship because the relationship itself is here to support the mission. Your lives are not here to support this relationship; the relationship is here to support the world."

"I know that both of you have wanted very much to feel that you had a glorious purpose on the earth, which indeed you have. But it has been nothing compared to the power that you will be able to feel through you, and through each other from this point forward."

Charles and I were positive that this would last until "death do us part". Many of the friends and family who watched were deeply moved by the promise behind Marianne's words, the ceremony itself and the love in the air. Certainly, we held the hope of many in the gathering that romantic fantasies can, and do, come true.

Suddenly I became aware that I was still sitting in my car in the midst of a howling storm. I shook off the memories of my dream wedding realizing that the fantasy did hold true for five great years. Then, without warning, it all began to unravel. I never would have believed we could grow apart. As we slipped away from each other, I reached for Charles in every way I knew; trying to pull him back, but it was like trying to hold back a wave in the ocean of another destiny. Our sex life began to wane and we spent our time doing different activities—always going our separate ways. To the outside world we maintained the illusion of unity, while we attempted to work out solutions. There were layers and layers of entanglements in the marriage, so many strands to be unraveled before the final tear. Because of our love and commitment to each other, it took over a year of attempted compromise, pain and insights to finally allow our paths to separate.

The storm continued to rage. This was probably not the best place to be day dreaming with branches and debris flying through the air all around my car. I shivered as a bolt of lightning shot through the sky highlighting what I knew in my heart, the partnership with Charles and the dream of a fairy tale marriage was lost to me. No matter how beautifully it had started out, no matter what others thought of my actions, no matter how much I wished it could continue, destiny had other plans for us. And like the storm, its outcome was both frightening and exciting.

Closing my eyes I prayed, "God, Oneness, All-That-Is, give me the strength and wisdom to continue to follow my inner guidance wherever it is leading. Give me the faith to trust the Universe to always support the highest good in every moment. With gratitude, I declare it so."

For now it was challenge enough to get from the car to my front porch. With a deep breath I picked up a sack of groceries, pulled the long strap of my purse over my head and pushed on the car door. I barely had the strength to swing it open against the driving wind and rain. By the time I ran the short distance to the front porch, my clothes were soaked through and my wet hair was sticking to my face and neck. As soon as I turned the door knob it flew open pushing the wind and rain into the house.

Throwing my sodden packages on the table, I forced the door closed and leaned against it as the storm amassed strength outside. Rain lashed against the glass of the wide picture window. Suddenly the world went black in a way that can only happen in the country, away from city lights, on a cloud covered night when the power goes out for miles in every direction.

I fumbled through the house muttering, "Where did I put that flashlight. I know I unpacked it. Maybe I can find the matches and candles somewhere in the kitchen."

Drawing a long breath, I fought to control my fear and remain upright rather than crumbling to the floor in tears. My heart pounded loudly and my stomach tightened as I worked my way along the wall into the kitchen and started a systematic search through recently filled drawers and cabinets. Finally I felt the flashlight. With that light I located my box of candles and some matches. Willing myself to relax, I began the process of lighting candles and spreading them throughout the downstairs. Trembling from my cold wet clothes and hair, I knew the fireplace was my next destination.

The warm blaze began to sooth me as I struggled to get a grip on my raw nerves. My stomach continued to tumble and tears of grief began to well up. How could I explain making such rash changes in my life for no apparent reason other than an inner voice that only I could hear, guiding my way?

I knew that my many friends and family would be supportive and attempt to understand even though they were sincerely perplexed over the breakup. I felt unable to explain my decisions to them, or to myself. It was important to maintain an open, clear channel to the guidance of my Spirit.

The unanswered questions remained. What was my Spirit telling me? Where was it leading me? Why did it require such a radical reorganization of my life?

The only thing for certain was that change was barreling down in my reality like a run-away train that could not be stopped.

I knew that I must surrender my life to my higher power and that fear could not take over my actions. I smiled to myself as I remembered that name of a book I once read, "Feel the Fear and Do it Anyway", by Susan Jeffers.

I had always felt that I was waiting for an invisible Light to awaken me, to call me out of an ordinary life and into my destiny. Even as a child, the world was unfamiliar to my way of being. When I was about five years old, I had a vivid, waking dream. I was walking down a wide hallway looking into individual cells displaying people playing out different roles in the human condition. There were family units, a mother and child, a husband and wife, friends, teams of people competing and many other relationships dramatized for my benefit. As I watched, I attempted to memorize the appropriate behavior of each relationship so that I could mimic life in a human body. None of it made any sense to me. Most of it seemed insane. Something inside of me, that was more real than the outer world around me, knew that I had my foundation in another place and that I was here on a mission that had not yet been revealed.

———————————

Snapping out of my reverie and drawing a long breath, I grabbed the flashlight to begin gathering blankets and pillows and prepare to rest, if sleep was even possible, on the couch. I put new logs on the fire, watching as it blazed with warmth and new hope. I kept telling myself that it was just a matter of waiting out the end of the storm and the coming of morning. Tomorrow was Sunday, my favorite day of the week. The local new-thought church where I was minister would be gathering, as always, to sing praise to the higher good in all of us.

Sighing, I closed my eyes hoping for slumber, but being bone tired didn't seem to make a difference. I had a wakeful night, a headache that never quite faded, and an emotional body filled with apprehension and fear of the unknown.

Morning arrived with gray skies, and more wind and rain. Childlike, I rubbed fists across sleep-deprived eyes and stumbled into the bathroom discovering, as I attempted to wash my face, that the power was still out. Thankfully, there were several gallons of water stored on the service porch and a propane camping stove in the garage. Hot coals remained in the fireplace giving the living room a semi-cozy feeling in the shadow of dawn. Grabbing my loafers and a coat from the mud room, I made my way to the garage to scrounge for supplies and feed the barn cats. Who knew how long the power would be out in this rural area?

Unstable emotions were stirring again. Walking back to the house, I wondered, "Why is it that women feel so helpless without the security of a man when faced with physical challenges. Is it because our bodies are not as strong . . . or is it something deeper, something on a more primal level?"

I remembered years ago, before my marriage to Charles, having lunch with Marianne Williamson and saying to her, "I don't know why I am never satisfied with the men in my life. Or why I end up having to leave because I start feeling like I am being smothered!"

She looked over and said, "It's because you always choose the same type of man, so you get the same results."

"No, I don't!" I had exclaimed. "You know the last three guys I dated. They were all totally different types in age, looks, and personalities; not at all the same. Why do you see them as alike?"

"They had one thing in common. None of them were capable of giving you what you want," Marianne replied.

The truth of that statement hit me like a ton of bricks. Of course that was true. Inwardly I wanted someone who shared my spiritual path and who had the same fascination with realizing our full soul potential together. None of my previous relationships were capable of satisfying that yearning because they lacked the ability, or inner awareness, to gratify that desire. Although Charles was always supportive, over time I went down a different spiritual path; one in which he could not join me.

I had thought Charles and I were in agreement about the reasons and circumstances of our separation, but years later Charles told me that his memory was quite different from mine. In his memory, after a few weeks of bickering, I walked down the stairs toward him one morning saying that I had figured out what was going on between us; "we are complete".

I was stunned when I realized Charles had experienced our final year together so differently. He thought I had just thrown our marriage away in a matter of a few weeks, while my truth was that it took over a year. Charles was quick to point out that everyone filters life through their own truth or perception of events. True to his generous personality, he expressed that he accepted the differences and knew it was the right choice for us. Every turn in the road gets us to where we are right now.

As I neared the back door after feeding the cats, a car drove up the gravel driveway with a familiar voice shouting over the sound of the wind, "Hello, Danielle. Are you alright?"

Looking around the side of the house I saw the smiling, handsome face of Donovan as he parked his car. He leaned out his window beside his barking dog, Max. The two of them were exactly what I needed to pull me back from the edge of despair.

"Hi, Dono! It is so great to see you. Come on in." I replied.

His grin widened as he stepped out of the car, grabbing Max by the collar before he could make his escape. They ran for the back door, Max jumping through puddles and Donovan laughing at his antics. Dono handed me Max's leash and turned to run back to the car where he grabbed the bag from the passenger seat. As I watched, I found myself relaxing the tension in my shoulders that had been building for days. Looking into Donovan's face everything seemed so blissfully normal again.

Donovan and his wife, Juelle, were a spiritual brother and sister to me. We met five years earlier in Sedona, Arizona at a retreat and had immediately recognized our strong connection. It was unusual for me to find a couple that I related to equally—they were like one being in separate bodies. To be with either, or both of them, was like standing in a warm, glowing light of love. Even their physical appearance seemed cloaked in light; both had blond hair, brilliant blue eyes and smiles as permanent fixtures on their beautifully tanned faces. Dono's sun energy was the perfect remedy for my unease and for this dreary weather.

A chuckle escaped my lips, as we entered the kitchen. "What is in the bag?" I asked.

"Max and I were on our way home from picking up our Sunday morning espresso and figured you could use one too. The power is out in most of the surrounding area except for downtown Chehalis. The roads are pretty clear considering the strength of the winds last night. Juelle and I were wondering if church is going to be canceled today."

"That reminds me. How did you get past the fallen tree on my road?"

"Looks like someone cut away enough to get through; maybe a neighbor? Luckily it just missed hitting any power lines."

I smiled into my coffee as I watched him pacing around the kitchen; Max at his heals waiting for a hand out of sweet pastries. Grabbing a donut out of the bag, Dono demanded, "Max, sit!"

Max's whole body began to wiggle with anticipation. Finally, he was able to control his excitement enough to plop down and look up with big brown eyes. Grinning, Donovan dropped the sweet into Max's smiling mouth. It was gone in an instant.

"It seems like a good day for church, even if only a few people show up. What do you and Juelle think?" I asked. Juelle acted as co-minister and was an integral part of the church service.

"We're with you. After all, we live in the Pacific Northwest where rain is a way of life. Juelle warned me not to stay too long so I better get a move on. We just wanted to be sure you weathered the storm." Dono was always a man of few words and short visits.

With laughter in my eyes, I walked toward Donovan for a hug. As always, his first reaction was to back away from physical contact, even though he knew I would just press in.

I was raised the only girl with two mischievous brothers and had always embraced the opportunity to tease them in retaliation for being on the receiving end so often.

Getting in a hug from a resisting Donovan had become a delightful game reminding me of my family dynamics. I could see Donovan's thought process clearly in his eyes, "I might as well get this over with." His strategy was to make it as quick as possible.

After a reluctant embrace, he grabbed Max and escaped to his car, shouting over his shoulder, "We'll see you in a couple of hours at the church, Danielle. We're bringing a couple of guests who are new to the area. They're our kind of people."

I felt a new charge run through my body. "My life is clicking back into gear", I thought, "and for the first time in over a year a whole new chapter is opening up." I felt ready to embrace it.

Picking up my coffee and blessing Dono's thoughtfulness, I rushed upstairs to get ready for church. Putting on black wool slacks and wool blazer with a red cashmere sweater, I stood in front of the mirror to apply eye makeup, a splash of color on my cheeks and lip gloss before grabbing my coat and purse to head out to the car. It was still raining but the wind had died down considerably.

Because of the fallen trees over the area, it took a while to get to the church using back roads which gave my active mind plenty of time to contemplate. I knew there had to be order in the world, a method to the universe. Throughout my years, I had often felt the guardianship of my spiritual family, those who had been with me on a journey toward Self discovery. My own alternative lifestyle was a testimony to having been watched over by higher forces of the other realms. In looking back, I could see that time and again my choices had been made from an inner knowing that was beyond understanding, leading to a life that was being orchestrated from somewhere outside of this reality; a life steeped in spiritual richness.

Chapter Two

Recognition

"Anyone in a state of seeking can never be happy.
Only those who are constantly finding are fulfilled.
And finding is not something that happens to us—
it is something we do."
~Alan Cohen~

I watched as Juelle and Donovan approached the entrance to the church sanctuary with a tall man and petite, attractive woman. I recognized the man from a channeling event in Sedona, Arizona several months before, but could not remember his name. Although he and I had spent four days in a room with only a couple dozen people, we had never spoken. My memory of him was that he sat very quietly in the back row with a golden light around him, while I was in my usual position in the front row with lots to say.

This morning he was dressed, as he had been in Sedona, in clothing that made him look as if he was going to a Star Trek convention—deep blue, indigo and silver colors with large shoulder pads and harem style pants that flared out at the thigh coming in tight at the ankle. He was wearing a pin over his heart shaped like a large symbol from another world—a gold triangle with a silver circular piece supporting an oblong raw crystal in the middle.

On most anyone else this would have looked very odd; however, on his tall, good looking frame and with his regal bearing they were somehow perfect. Donovan, also tall and handsome, wore his version of this clothing style with the same affect. The two of them walking together was a sight to behold.

I was familiar with this clothing line. It was popular with people who attended the seminars with Earth Mission in Sedona. Although some women seemed drawn to it, men were especially attracted. The designers considered clothing to be a form of expression that carried with it certain spiritual frequencies and, from my experiences, they may be right.

I reflected back to a time when I had accompanied my friend, Craig, on his first adventure with this line of clothing. We went to the home of the designers, Jacob and Sarina, in Sedona, Arizona.

They explained, "The clothing and jewelry we work with is a spiritual technology—not simply apparel. While they appear to be beautiful bright costumes, they are much more than that. Our clothing is programmed to transform and exalt higher frequencies both in the individuals who wear them and those who look upon them."

The first outfit Craig put on consisted of bright yellow cotton harem pants and a matching unisex tunic top with a large broach made from gold and silver resins and featuring a quartz crystal in the center. Immediately Craig seemed altered in some way. It was as if he were being outfitted for an appearance in the celestial realms. Obviously this was not a simple dress-up party.

The fitting/transformation session went on for about an hour. Some of the outfits worked their magic in just a few moments—taking Craig to the next level. Then it was time to change into another outfit. Exhilaration and energy seemed to flow through his body with each change of clothes. He described it as being adjusted by a sequence of body work specialists.

Before leaving, Sarina and Jacob led Craig through a process that assisted him in seeing his multi-dimensional identity for the first time. He was asked to close his eyes and relax while they led him on a journey by way of his imagination, inviting him to meet himself in a higher spiritual awareness. He had not anticipated the intensity and magnitude of his transformation and walked out feeling both dazed and exalted.

––––––––––––––

Bringing my attention back to the here and now, I made eye contact with the man before me, noting hazel/green eyes above a faintly aristocratic straight nose and full lips. His thinning, dark, soft curly hair fell to his shoulders in the back. He carried himself like a holy man with the confidence of knowing he was both different and special; a prince from another dimension.

"Hi, we made it!" Juelle said with her infectious smile. "We brought two wonderful new friends who are traveling through. This is Qua and Terri. Meet Danielle."

"Welcome. We are always happy to have new faces join our Sunday gathering. Qua, weren't we together at the Earth Mission event in Arizona a couple of months ago?"

A new light shown in Qua's remarkable eyes and after a moment he said, "Yes, I do remember you now. I did not put the name with your face when Juelle told us about your church. Good to see you again."

Qua gave me a stiff hug—one of those where only your shoulders meet and the contact is broken as quickly as possible. A quick judgment ran through my head, "Hum, this guy is pretty uptight."

I turned my attention to Terri, a vivacious woman with a sparkle in her cherub-like face; a face framed by a wild mane of short hair. Her laughter bubbled out as I moved forward for a full-body squeeze from her petite-frame.

I was immediately enchanted with her open nature and childlike enthusiasm. We fell into easy conversation and laughter as if we'd known one another for years.

Looking at them I wondered, "Since they are obviously traveling together, it is likely that they are in an intimate relationship, or they might even be married? However, their body language is very distant from one another. Everything is not as it seems," I thought, "Not that it matters to me."

Shaking off my habit of becoming preoccupied with speculation on subjects that were none of my concern, I moved on to greet the next group arriving. I loved the variety of people who attended our church. We were open to and honored all religions, welcoming a broad spiritual spectrum.

Much to the amazement of many, Charles, my soon to be former husband, was still an active participant in the church. We remained very close friends even though there was an uncomfortable undercurrent that we could not totally overcome this early in our transition. We each sought a level of detachment, while keeping our hearts open to one another, so that we would have enough emotional distance to find out what was real and how to best reform our relationship. I felt that we had been destined to be partners for a purpose greater than ourselves and that it had run its course.

———————————

The only real choice we ever had was how long to spend in this specific form of marriage and how and when to change it. I have observed that it is common for people to continue in marriages long after the form has stopped supporting growth and personal destiny. Many wait until their relationship is so uncomfortable that they must leave, usually with great pain and anger.

Charles and I had the courage and conviction not to let love, respect and honor get destroyed by trying to protect the "form" of our relationship. Our wedding vows to one another were to live in support of a higher Truth beyond ourselves. In our case I was clear that the marriage must be dissolved in order to become all that we could be, individually. I did not know all the reasons, but it was obvious to me that living together as husband and wife was creating constraints on our personal growth. When we spent a lot of time together, we were feeling "less" rather than "more". We needed more distance in order to fully support each other and we were willing to flow with this personally painful change rather than resist it by holding on.

Looking toward the entrance to the church, I noticed Charles walking through the front door, as always surrounded by people wanting to bathe in his warmth and charm. I waved a greeting and turned to walk with Juelle into the sanctuary. Despite last night's storm and the persistent wind and rain, the chairs were filled with familiar and new faces. Juelle and I took our places beside the altar and began the service with a prayer of gratitude and deep commitment to surrendering as a group into service to God/Oneness/All-That-Is.

As the prayer ended and the congregation started to sing "Only Here for God", I felt the familiar euphoric feelings that filled me every Sunday as the joined energy of the congregation created a sacred space. It was as if the Christ energy entered my body and took over, speaking through me as I, the ego, stepped aside. From the moment I first stood in front of groups as a minister, I was able to access a powerful force deep inside that was magical and mysterious, with great wisdom and knowledge and definitely beyond my personality. During those illuminated moments I knew that my actions were being orchestrated by Spiritual energies with a specific purpose for each individual in the group.

I was aware that I could easily articulate divine truths and captivate an audience, but today, as I looked out on the congregation, I noted a look of skepticism on Qua's face. Clearly, church did not appear to be his thing nor, for that matter, did he appear to like me very much. My mind wandered back to that reluctant hug as he and Terri entered this morning. "Not only uptight" I thought, "but some kind of introvert who doesn't trust easily. Obviously, we're miles apart in temperament. It would be tough being friends with this guy."

As the hour long service was coming to an end, the congregation formed a circle, held hands and began to sing the closing song. The energy of the group was a level that went beyond personal to the only perfect Love—a soul connection. No strangers existed in this moment; the invisible strands of individual suffering and separation had been broken.

I looked around the circle of beautiful faces, young and old, big and small, women and men all committed to their own unique journey toward finding their way back to embracing their true identity—spiritual beings inhabiting a human body. For me, these moments were the ones I lived to experience. I knew that the Ministry was my true calling. My curiosity about people and their potential drove my life. My fascination with who they were, what they expected out of life, what they dreamed of, defined my ministry. Watching people awaken to their own magnificence was my greatest joy.

For one illuminating moment, my eyes fell on Qua. Utterly shocked after my observations of him, I experienced a stunning feeling of awareness. The connection seemed ancient, a buried memory. It needed no words. It was like a powerful force deep inside—magical and profoundly sacred. As I broke eye contact, a mood of peacefulness fell over me even as my mind asked, "What just happened!"

The congregation moved from the sanctuary to the outer meeting room still basking in the warmth of the service. The room was crowded making it obvious that the church would need to find a larger space to congregate. We only had one more week left on our lease. During announcements that morning, Juelle and I had asked for volunteers to form a committee of twelve people to meet at my home the next evening to discuss options open to us. Both Qua and Terri were among the people who agreed to attend.

"Hey, Danielle," Donovan called from across the room. "Come on. We're all headed out to lunch at that new Mexican restaurant."

Knowing I still had unpacking to do, I responded, "Thanks anyway, Dono. I better get home and start the fire in case the power is still out. Have fun! See you tomorrow evening at my house for the church council meeting."

Leaving behind a few volunteers to clean up and knowing that Charles would lock the church, I headed for my car planning to make a stop at my favorite store. I knew it was the personal touches that would make my new house feel like a home—fresh flowers, the smell of candles and food, the sounds of a crackling fire, music and friends.

Navigating the country roads, I met crews out in mass cleaning up after the worst of the storm and getting ready for the Monday commute, such as it was in this rural Washington town. Arriving back at the house, I looked around and realized for the first time that this little farm suited me perfectly with its front porch, old barn and beautiful established bulbs, flowers and trees. I was looking forward to spring when it would all wake from its winter slumber, and I could experience the quiet satisfaction of watching the first buds blossom into new life. It felt like an apt time of the year for my own new beginnings.

In a desire to calm my fears, I had forgotten that plans can be useful and entertaining; however, life has too many surprises to take plans too seriously.

My destiny was beyond my ability to know. The conscious mind can seldom, if ever, foresee what is for the highest good. My task was to surrender into the journey, thereby aligning myself with a loving Universe. Life will always play itself out in harmony with higher Truth, no matter how it looks from an earthly or third dimensional perspective.

Little did I know that my life was about to go in a new direction that was very different from the one I thought was my destiny.

Chapter Three

Visionary Dream

"The universe is full of magical things,
patiently waiting for our wits to grow sharper."
~Eden Phillpotts~

By the time evening fell, I was exhausted and ready to take a break from my mad dash to create a homey atmosphere. Wearing comfortable leggings and an over-sized T-shirt, I stretched out on the couch and rubbed a hand over the tense spot in the back of my neck and shoulders. A blazing fire added warmth and beauty to my new home and fresh roses on the table beside the couch complimented the scene. Candlesticks with tapers burning down to varying heights were placed around the room.

The sights, smells and sounds of home filled my senses with bliss. I loved the way the moonlight slanted through tall fir trees and danced through the large picture window. I sighed, closed my eyes, and enjoyed the feeling of heat on my cheeks from the crackling fire. Now that the house was clean, warm and things were in their place, I could finally relax. The only additions needed to complete my bliss were my horses. But that would have to wait until I could fix up the old abandoned barn on the property. In the meantime, I would enjoy the opportunity to take regular riding lessons on Kalypso, my gelding, who was being boarded with my trainer. During these storms, it was reassuring to know that he was being well cared for.

I thought of my daughters, Shannon living outside of Olympia, Washington and Alex attending college in Pasadena, CA. and smiled to myself. Oh, how they would tease me looking conspiratorially at each other, "Mom is doing that 'Martha Stewart' thing again." After which they would break into delighted giggles.

Those close to me had often accused me of being too much of a perfectionist and suggested that I ease up on my need to control. And I have to admit they were correct, every time I attempted to sit down and relax I would think of the never ending things still left to be done. Restlessness would have me up, my mind ordering me not to waste time. My ego could run me ragged, with its constant nagging, "Danielle, make sure the gardening is done, the lawn mowed, the animals fed and the house is aesthetically perfect. Someone might stop by, so be sure there is food and drink to serve." . . . and on and on it went."

My entire life had been focused on doing my utmost and being my best. That, I had always believed, was who I was; a product of my heredity, my upbringing; and my own stringent standards for myself. The problem was that my inner joy, rhythm and guidance were all too often sacrificed in my attempts to live up to this perfect world I felt responsible to create.

Remembering my mind's habit of constant chatter, I consciously became quiet and relaxed into a feeling of peace, enjoying the moment just as it was. I reflected on what brought me to this crossroad in my life.

For as long as I could remember, much of my attention and energy had been taken up in accommodating others. In truth, it felt fantastic to be alone, completely on my own, in this quiet, peaceful room. Without anyone's needs to consider, life was less complicated and emotionally draining. I no longer had the time, inclination or energy for an intimate relationship. I reasoned that if Charles and I could not stay together, the hope of 'happily ever after' was

not in my destiny. I was looking forward to the next phase of my life and was
quite sure that it would be primarily committed to my church and spiritual
work. Now that my daughters were grown, it felt off-purpose to waste time on
the drama of a relationship that could easily take away from my ability to be
available to serve as a minister. I knew that with all of my complexities, my
strengths and weaknesses, my only meaningful purpose in life was to grow and
assist others in growing spiritually.

My phone rang bringing me back into present time.

"Hello."

"Hi Danielle, this is Michaela. How are you doing? I heard that you and Charles are separated. I'm so surprised and sorry to hear it. You always seemed so perfect for each other."

"Thanks. We're really just fine. I think, on some levels, this has been more difficult for other people than for Charles or me. Our love and support for each other is still strong. We're just not living together anymore."

"I trust that you will do what is best" Michaela exclaimed. "I called Juelle to get your new telephone number because I'm planning to drive up to treat chiropractic patients in your area next week on Tuesday. Since my last patient is quite late, I was wondering if it would be OK if I stayed with you that one night. Do you have room for me?"

"Sure Michaela. I'd love to see you. We can catch up then. You'll be my first house guest. I'm just settling in to my new place just a few minutes north of Chehalis but have a pull-out couch which is reasonably comfortable."

Michaela was a Chiropractor and Acupuncturist who came up from her home in Portland, Oregon on occasion to treat long-time patients and attend spiritual events. Although we did not know each other well, I always found her fascinating. She was a very accomplished woman with a strong mental body that was fighting for control in conflict with her more powerful spiritual essence—pushing herself toward the brink of new awakenings that went beyond the mind. I felt that Michaela would soon join me in surrendering into the unknown leading her on a path toward her unique divine destiny. It is my belief that no one can live in two worlds for long; eventually they must tip one way or the other. The choice is simple, either the individual has a personal identity primarily as a spiritual being with focused awareness in this moment, or primarily as a human being living through thoughts of the past and future.

"Great, I'll see you around 10:00 p.m. a week from this Tuesday." Michaela said.

"I'll be home so don't worry about the time. Just show up when you are ready. And, Michaela, there is no reason to be concerned about Charles and me; everything is good. I'll fill you in next week."

Hanging up the phone and relaxing back on the couch, I huddled under my covers preparing to read a book by the flickering firelight. The darkness and ambiance were so peaceful.

With a blast of energy and sound, the power exploded into existence. It was as blindly sudden as the loss of power had been. After two days of having no electricity, my body and mind had become accustomed to the quiet; now the whole house seemed to have come alive with piercing energy. The refrigerator and heater fans were humming and lights throughout the house demanded attention.

"Well" I thought, "I guess my attempt at sitting down and doing nothing is at an abrupt end. There is the water heater to re-light, the clocks to set and food in the refrigerator to throw away before carrying my exhausted body to bed!"

My mind, back to its old tricks, gave me a continuous list of things I should do before relaxing. In an attempt to break this pattern of running on raw adrenalin, I attended to the safety necessities and then consciously stopped all activity, walking up the stairs to my bedroom and allowing my body to sink into bed before complete exhaustion took over. All the things that needed to be done, according to my mind, could wait a little while longer.

With the tensions of the last days draining away and with an exhausted mind, I moved into the silence of an unknown earth time, sleeping deeply.

Remembering

Wearing a white glazed robe of shimmering pastels, I walked alone surrounded by the sound of tiny unseen bells. Without fear I moved, as if floating, through an iridescent mist of swirling energy. Gradually the sound of water gently moving over stone permeated my consciousness and I became aware of the scent of multitudes of flowers.

From directly before me came the sound of bells, deeper in tone and complimenting the gentle sounds surrounding my progress. Alert now to change, my senses began to cartwheel into one another with anticipation. The mist seemed to thin and a figure, wearing a long robe made of very soft translucent material flowing gracefully with each movement, came toward me. Masculine energy emanated from the figure; he was tall with a regal bearing. As he drew nearer, we were surrounded by the soft sound of toning from many voices.

His eyes, so filled with love, looked directly into my soul and I into his.

My breathing slowed, deepening as if in a trance state. The mist around us began to dance; the air moving through our bodies was thick with the sweetness of nectar.

Mesmerized by the love in this man's eyes, I reach up to frame his face with my hands. At the moment my hands touched his glowing skin, my consciousness soared while the dancing particles of my body began to merge with his. We dissolved into each other. Where there had been two there was now one. This man and I, acting as one, began to vibrate; like the strings of one harp. Within the swirling mist still surrounding us, we gently began to rotate, as if dancing together, in a clockwise motion—one with the mist, yet apart from it. Our speed increased beyond that of vision and we separated from the rainbow mist becoming a storm of swirling brilliant golden energy reaching up and out as far as could be perceived and beyond.

———————

I became aware of a floating sensation, my awareness returning from a distant unknown place. Opening my eyes I saw, without seeing, the fir trees swaying outside my window. At some level, I knew my location, but my mind and body dwelled, still, in the energy of the amazing experience.

It was more than pleasure. It was beyond any vision ever held in my imagination, any dream ever held in my heart. It was true, unconditional love for all of creation. It was a glimpse of life through the Eyes of Divinity. It was a merging I had been looking for, without knowing it, all my life.

I reluctantly came back into awareness as the warm haze over my mind cooled like a hallucinogenic drug. I wished only to stay in bed, still immersed in the sensations and glorying in every breath, as love poured out through every cell in my body. Never had I felt such unrestricted, complete abandonment of all worry and fear.

I ran my hands over my body, luxuriating in the feel of being alive. It was 5:30 a.m. I was now fully awake, yet the dream was as real as if it had happened in an awakened state. My awareness of it was more vivid than anything that had ever happened in my experience.

My intuition told me that this visionary dream had set into motion a series of events that would change the course of my life.

Chapter Four

Council Meeting

"Ninety-nine percent of who you are is
invisible and untouchable."
~Buckminster Fuller~

Unsure of my reality, I crawled out of bed in a dazed state, and headed for the bathroom. Drawing water into my claw foot tub, I filled it lavishly with oil and sank into it with a long sigh. A surge of gratitude for running hot water, wonderful smelling bath oils and the time to enjoy them filled me. Luxuriating, I smoothed frothy bubbles down my legs and arms. After a long soak, I stepped out of the tub, let the water drain, toweled off slowly and creamed my skin with the delicious smell of mint.

Still immersed in my dream, I dressed in jeans and a soft blue sweater and went downstairs for a light breakfast. Nothing seemed the same—the world around me sparkled with new life and energy.

As time went on, a mood of peacefulness teetered against the thoughts racing in my mind. What did the dream mean? Was this a joining of the male and female aspects of myself into a cohesive whole? Did I marry myself?

All at once I recognized the man in my dreams. He was the friend of Juelle and Donovan's who attended church yesterday. I was startled, but within moments realized that it was not unusual for me to have someone I knew, even a movie star, play a part in my dreams. Certainly this was not a personal statement about Qua. I barely knew him, and we did not seem to have any personal connection.

I spent the rest of the day preparing for the evening council meeting to determine how to expand into the next phase of the church.

At 7:00 p.m. sharp the first group arrived.

"Hi, come on in and make yourselves at home. We have drinks and snacks in the kitchen. We'll place the chairs in a circle after everyone arrives."

"Wow, your new home is great. It is so warm and inviting!" Charlene gushed as she walked through the door. "Look at this wonderful country kitchen, and I just love the yard, at least the little I could see in the dark!"

"Thanks." I replied in a distracted voice. Despite the activities of the day, I was still filled with the memory and wonder of my dream. So much so that I felt I needed to discuss it with someone. Any other conversation seemed irrelevant right now.

Walking over to my good friend, Claudia, I asked, "Could we talk for a moment?"

"Sure" Claudia replied

"I had a very vivid, visionary dream this morning that has stayed with me all day. I feel I must tell someone about it to see if its message will become clearer to me. When I looked at you just now, I knew you are the one to share with."

"Sounds enticing. Let's hear it."

I told her the story, easily going back through the experience. Claudia was mesmerized. She stood there, tears running freely down her face as she listened.

When I finished she spoke quietly, "I feel as if my soul has lost all connections from layer after layer of hurt and doubt around relationships. I've been afraid to allow myself to release the walls I've built to protect myself from the pain of allowing another person in close. Something happened deep inside as I listened to your vision. It feels like a crack has been made in my wall that will, eventually, tear it down permanently. Thank you. I feel so blessed!"

The look in her tear-filled eyes was a stunning moment. I could see that the Light had pierced through her suffering and pain. We hugged, and then pulled away, continuing to hold eye contact for a moment—knowing that we had connected from a place where no one is a stranger to anyone else. Emotion was pouring through me like fine wine; I experienced a knowingness that at every moment each person has an opportunity to awaken through our invisible strands of interconnectedness.

A knock on the door interrupted the connection between Claudia and me. I excused myself and went to greet a new arrival.

In the meantime Qua was parking his car in front of my house and saw that Terri, who must have arrived earlier with Juelle, was waiting outside on the porch.

"Hi. I thought I'd wait for you before going in."

"Has it already started? You must be cold out here." Qua said as he stepped up beside Terri.

"I'm O.K. It is a little cold," she said with a flirtatious smile. "Everyone's just getting here."

Later Qua told me that he was not sure why he was attending this meeting. He knew he was not attracted to this area as a home base. He had come to connect with Juelle and Donovan and had plans to leave this cold, wet Washington winter weather and head south very soon.

Shivering after the warmth of his car Qua said, "Let's get inside out of the cold."

———————————

I was standing in a small group, still feeling immersed in the energy I had shared with Claudia. So strong was the sensation that I felt compelled once again to share my visionary dream with others. As I began, Qua and Terri entered the house and joined us. I described the experience of walking through an iridescent mist toward a robed individual. I shared the feeling of my body's dissolution into floating particles that merged with those of the male figure; the two, now one being, rotating and becoming a swirl of brilliant golden energy. Finally, I revealed that the person who played the male essence in my dream looked like Qua.

"Although," I added with a smile in his direction, "I do not think it is in any way personal to you, Qua."

As I continued with a description of the male essence and sounds of toning in my dream, I was aware of a faraway look on Qua's face. It was as if he had mentally left the planet. I wasn't sure what was happening inside him, however I sensed a deep reaction of some kind and recognized the symptoms of a person receiving information from beyond this world.

When I completed my story and returned to current space and time, I noticed Qua intensely looking at me with amazed curiosity; clearly he had input to be shared. It would have to wait until later as the group was beginning to gather in a circle for the council meeting.

It was apparent to those closest to me that I was in an altered state. Whenever I made eye contact with Qua, the energy vibrating between us was almost visible. With great effort, I forced myself to concentrate on the agenda of the gathering.

In the back of my mind I was thinking, "Just yesterday the future of the church was a very high priority in my life. Now it is difficult to think about it let alone make plans that would impact the lives of the congregation and set a path to my future. The only thing that is vivid in my reality right now is the vision and questions about Qua's reaction to it.

With a minimum of consciousness, I managed to get through the meeting and thank many long time supporters for participating. Looking around I realized that only three people were left, Qua, Terri and Emily. Qua walked over to me to ask if we could have a more private conversation.

"Sure," I said. "Is Terri going to wait or does she want to join us?"

"She wants to spend some time talking to Emily", he said as we moved to sit near the fireplace.

Without preamble and almost as if the words were tumbling from him, he began, "When you were describing your vision, I felt that the words were coded for me. As I listened to your description and experiences, time slowed, and then stopped. While my body remained with you and the group, I was no longer with the room full of people; it felt like I was in a haze. I entered a realm beyond time; that of the residence of my Councils as they prepared to send me a message."

I looked at him with surprise. Until that moment, it had not occurred to me that the male energy in my dream was in any way personally about Qua. As I let the possibility into my awareness, my face flushed, registering the truth that this experience had something to do with the two of us.

After a moment, I said, "O.K. I know we don't have much time to explore this right now, but I'd love to hear more about your councils."

"What I refer to as my council is a distinct feeling—like the sense you get when someone is standing behind you without touching or speaking. I sense the presence of eight entities sitting in an oval above my left shoulder and a few feet away. Their purpose has to do with networking and connecting humans, and their activities on Earth are on a subtle energy level.

My inner knowing is that the eight members represent new frequencies and possibilities not currently in abundance on Earth. It's very other-worldly in nature. I pondered a name that I could use to address this council, one that conveyed their frequency, character and demeanor. One of the descriptive words that came to mind was 'regal'. 'Royal Light' emerged from this. Then a word that I felt fit their mission and their method of networking and connecting groups and individuals—'Command'. So I call my council The Royal Light Command."

"Fascinating. May I ask another question? I've noticed that your clothes are often in a particular color range. Does that have anything to do with The Royal Light Command?"

"Yes. When I sense colors that resonate with the council as a single entity, I feel very deep blue or indigo and silvery white. The name, Royal Light Command, also feels in harmony with these colors. I have created symbols to give further expression to this Council because when described in words, it seems so odd and limited. I used sketching and automatic writing. Very quickly a symbol came through that felt authentic. In some multidimensional way, part of me is expressed as one of the eight members while another part of me is now in this human body."

As Qua spoke I could sense psychic energy flaring between us.

Qua continued, "At this point in my journey, my life is devoted to my mission. While I freely share companionship with others, I feel it is quite possible that I am destined to have a life without intimate personal relationships, so I'm not interpreting your vision to mean that we are to come together as man and woman."

I quickly concurred, "I totally agree. If this means anything about us, it must have something to do with our spiritual work."

Qua nodded in agreement and continued, "My fascination is with a higher spiritual interpretation. I wonder if we are destined to work together in some way, or if I am being asked to play a role in your church. No clear meaning or next steps are apparent, only that some significant change in my destiny is about to happen and it seems to include you in some way."

"Guess we'll have to continue this on another day. Terri is looking restless and ready to leave. Let's get together soon and explore the possibilities." I suggested.

Qua smiled his agreement, watching me as I consciously pulled myself away from this intriguing new development and refocused on completing the evening's activities.

We walked over to Emily and Terri to exchange our goodbyes.

Alone again, my attention turned to the significance of all that had happened since yesterday. "What was I to do about it? Perhaps nothing. Did the part that Qua played in my dream have more importance than I had previously thought? He seemed to have a fascinating story, but what had that to do with me? Were he and I supposed to support one another's mission in some significant way?"

Dropping down into an overstuffed chair, I began a relaxation exercise that usually quieted my mind. Not this time! The long established habit of control beckoned, but I knew that was a trap.

Asking for inner guidance to tell me the next step, my immediate answer was that a collaboration with Qua was a real possibility and I would be wise to pursue the possibilities.

Almost immediately, my mind took off again with its chatter back and forth. *"If I open the door to my mental reasoning, my inner voice may become too quiet to hear clearly over my mind's chatter. What has happened to my plans to back away from close relationships with any man and dedicate my full attention to being of service as a minister?*

I thought that I had reached a place in evolution where the most effective next step would to be to disengage from the small stories of life and live more fully in the sacred realms where I felt more removed from the worldly dramas. It seemed that too much time and energy had been spent dealing with personal issues. My marriage to Charles had been perfect in so many ways, yet I could not stay. Again, I asked, "Doesn't that mean that I am to live a monastic life with no close relationships so that my full attention is on service as a minister?"

I reflected back on a short relationship I had with Peter; my ultimate sexual fantasy. As in many romantic movies, we first met with eye contact across a crowded room and both experienced a powerful, magnetic jolt of physical awareness.

We were talking about making a life together from the first date. After about a month, we met at a remote cottage in Northern California for a weekend of sensual delight. The many doubts I had that we were meant to be together soon dissolved. Why else would our physical connection be so strong. Although I had been unaware of its existence, my subconscious mind had believed the romantic movies. I thought it was possible that some handsome, macho guy would see me and drop all of his philandering ways because he realized that I was 'the one'. And we would know this by our sexual attraction to each other.

Peter soon taught me differently. He was a master manipulator of women using their desire to be saved by a white knight with a great body. He played the part perfectly while his 'philandering ways' never slowed down for a moment. It was a great lesson; through inner work I was able to release that entire fantasy.

Bringing myself back from the memories, I shook my head and thought, *"Women are so conditioned to jump to conclusions when we are dealing with an attractive man, and think it will lead to intimacy. Here I am worrying about compromising my monastic life when most likely there is a project that Qua and I are supposed to do together."*

One thing was clear, Qua somehow was going to play a vital part in my future. But what? There was no logical answer, not even many options. The only thing to do was to make contact and see what he experienced when I shared my vision.

With a sigh of relief at that conclusion, I decided to call Qua the next day and arrange for a meeting to explore the possibilities.

Chapter Five

Qua and Terri

"Nothing real can be threatened.
Nothing unreal exists.
Therein lies the peace of God."
~A Course in Miracles~

In the meantime Qua was having his own experience:
After leaving the meeting, Terri and Qua drove back to her house, silence stretching between them. Terri seemed lost in her own world while Qua sat in deep thought reflecting on their journey together.

For the last few months, they had been living in an RV or staying with friends. It was not clear at all what the future of their relationship was to be. A little less than a year ago, he met Terri hoping to find a more casual relationship—a female friend, who shared at least some of his spiritual values.

As they sat together in a coffee shop, even before they were deeply into their first conversation, Qua had a vision of fleeting, colored shapes that flew about

Terri's head and off into the distance. Such visions were quite common for him at that time in his life, and they certainly got his attention and challenged him to draw some kind of meaning from them. In his experience, the meanings were left in the mystery and he resisted the temptation to read too much into them, rather he tried to relax into appreciation for simply being given opportunities to peek into other realities.

The whimsical vision of pastel geometric shapes around Terri's head seemed to reflect her lightness of being and sense of humor. They began seeing more of each other, and later, she joined him when he left his home, job and friends in search of his next spiritual assignment. Because it was like stepping into the void, trusting in the universe to show him the way and provide whatever was needed to survive and flourish, a companion was most welcome.

During their travels, his awareness of new spiritual realities grew in strength. The unencumbered lifestyle removed the familiar human contexts and allowed new insights and awareness to flood into his awareness. One evening in the RV, as Qua was writing a letter to a friend, he was overcome by an intense feeling of stillness and bliss. He continued his letter and the English words on the page progressed into cryptic syllables, a kind of gibberish that somehow made sense to him. Embedded in the letters was the name Qua Tua'. He immediately recognized it as his name from a higher frequency of his true identity.

As he sat looking at the page, his body and breath felt frozen in time while Divine Grace was slowly pouring over him from above like a warm enveloping liquid. During the experience Qua could neither speak nor move, but silently witnessed the celestial transformation. He felt a shift in his essence, a new identity, that was instantly gentler, humble and, yes, more wise.

There were new insights and knowing available to him after this transcendental experience, although over time the intensity gradually subsided. As hours and days passed, he gained some ability to express and share what had happened.

Qua's former inner identity had been replaced by a new, expanded, and a much more magnificent sense of being. He had been a human on a rather bold spiritual quest. Now he was an adventurer from enlightened realms exploring human experiences. Nothing looked or felt the same.

———————————

From the beginning, Terri had been maneuvering toward marriage and commitment, perhaps more than she realized or admitted. Qua loved her as a spiritual being and a companion; however, he did not see her as a life partner. She delighted him with her humor and amazed him with her artistic abilities. The two of them had been very childlike together, dancing inside their RV to 30's big band music, exploring the countryside, and not planning for the future.

Now Qua felt a distance between them, the kind of growing apart that normally comes after years of being in a dysfunctional relationship. But instead of years, his transformation brought this about in hours.

Intimate interactions with Terri had already waned as the difference in their life goals became more apparent. Terri began to strategize ways to bring them back to their previous relationship with candle light dinners, laughter and attempts to be a part of Qua's fast paced spiritual journey.

Unlike most men, he did not measure relationships based merely on chemistry and personal attraction. Even though Qua felt, from the beginning, that Terri and he were on a journey together for a limited amount of time, his primary interest was their spiritual connection and it had been diminishing. He found himself being the teacher instead of a partner. This, and the shifts from his 'download', manifested itself in his lack of sexual attraction toward her. Qua's inner spiritual assignment had changed and he knew that Terri was no longer a significant part of it. Terri's self esteem was suffering and Qua's conditioned human reaction was to pull even further away, adding fuel to the fire and creating a serious downward spiral.

Qua had been in Sedona the previous week. During the trip, it became clear that he needed to make the break with Terri. He felt a sense of urgency to broach the subject of separation as soon as possible.

Donovan picked him up from the airport when he returned to Washington from Sedona. Qua wondered where Donovan was taking him since he did not recognize the route. "Possibly a back way to his house where I had been staying," he thought.

"There is a surprise waiting for you." Dono had said.

"Is that why we seem to be going somewhere other than your house?" Qua had asked.

"You'll see soon enough" Dono said with a chuckle. "The women have been up to something again."

They drove up to a rustic little farm house and Qua recognized his motor home sitting in the front but there were no other cars. He thought, "Oh no, did Terri rent this house without telling me. Is this my surprise! How am I going to let her know that I am not planning to live here?"

"Well, here we are! I've been instructed to let you off here and disappear."

"Thanks for the ride." Qua murmured, not wanting to show his concern to Donovan. Qua grabbed his suitcase and walked toward the house, hearing Donovan behind him as he turned his car around and drove away down the country road.

As Qua entered the front door, the scene that met him was both romantic and welcoming. Terri had completely cleaned, painted and moved into the house putting in hours of work. The results were stunning with bright, bold colors, overstuffed furniture, flowers, and candles glowing on tables topped off with the smell of fresh baked chocolate chip cookies.

Terri greeted him with a glass of wine and a look of delight in her eyes "Isn't this just amazing! I didn't want to tell you about it on the phone. I wanted it to be a surprise!"

Qua's heart fell. In that environment, he could not bring himself to share his feelings honestly.

At times like this Qua would remember what a relationship therapist told him when he sought counseling a few years before. He was seeking to discover why he felt unfulfilled in personal relationships, as well as the significance of visions he was having.

After several deep sessions and explorations, she said, "Oh, I see. You are not actually available for relationships with women because you are already in an intimate relationship with God. You do not have room for a woman in your life as a significant, long-term partner."

At the time Qua experienced an epiphany at the truth of this statement and relaxed into living solo.

Bringing his awareness back to the present, Qua saw that he and Terri had arrived back at her house after the council meeting. He knew it was past time to have an honest talk. It was not fair to either of them to go on pretending. Having lived through a childhood of emotional episodes with his mother and sister, he was not looking forward to this conversation. Since the occurrence in the RV, Qua was experiencing profound spiritual clarity and connection yet finding it difficult to relate in the 'human' side of being in a body with all of its mental chatter and confusing thoughts.

"Want a snack or some tea?" Terri asked, breaking the silence between them.

"Sure."

At the sound of his voice, emotions began to rise in Terri's entire body. Although Qua's tone was soft, something told her that they were about to open up feelings they had both been avoiding. She pushed them down again and put on a cheerful smile, busily preparing their snack.

Qua walked into the kitchen avoiding eye contact and began helping her. With hands full they sat down at the small kitchen table across from each other. She gazed at him with a multitude of emotions flitting over her face before blindly looking down.

Qua's body stiffened uncomfortably. "Terri, I did a lot of thinking while I was away last week", he began. "This whole house thing is just not the direction that is right for me. I am truly touched that you did so much work making this a home, but it is not for me. We started out on an adventure together to explore our next steps and it looks like this is where you have landed."

Terri pressed her fingers to her eyes fighting for something to say that would convince him that they could have a great life together. Taking a deep, but quivering breath Terri began, "We don't have to stay here. It is just a month-to-month rental. I thought you liked this community and we could settle down for a while. But if you don't want to . . ."

"Terri", Qua interrupted, "all forms of relationships have a beginning, middle and an end. Forms do not last forever, they are always changing. We have been approaching the end of this form in our relationship for a while now. I think you've felt it as much as I have; we've talked about how our feelings have shifted over the past few months. I still care for you, but it no longer feels appropriate to travel or live together. No one is at fault and there is nothing either of us can do to change it. I know it is not comfortable but we can figure it all out and move on with as little pain as possible."

Her throat caught as Terri spoke in a trembling voice, "How can you sit there and act like I'm a stranger? How can you throw away the life and dreams we built together?"

"I didn't set out to hurt anyone. I would never willingly hurt you. That's not my intention", Qua said. "This is destiny; something beyond either of us. We are being called in different directions. It really isn't personal."

Qua reached out to touch Terri's hand.

She jerked back and pushed him away, "What do you mean it isn't personal! I wanted to believe you were just on a journey last week and would come back to me. I felt your distance but couldn't say anything to you and I was so lonely. We get along great. To me you are wonderful, **we** are wonderful together, but just this moment I have seen how uncaring you can be. It feels very personal to me."

With every word from Terri the distance between her and Qua widened. They had, Qua realized, resolved nothing when it came to mutual understanding—only opened deep wounds and distortional fears. Terri's hands were covering her face, her shoulders heaving—helpless, hopeless tears.

Qua stood, walked over to her and spoke softly, "Terri, come on, it's getting late. Why don't you go upstairs to bed, get some sleep and we will talk more in the morning."

Appearing too tired, too bruised to come up with a strategy to turn things around, Terri walked out of the room. She had the look of a woman experiencing an age-old ache in her heart; one that Qua's spiritual wisdom was not going to penetrate. Terri didn't want his wisdom, she wanted him.

Qua felt confused by the fact that Terri continued to cling. It forced him into a position of appearing to reject her when his true intent was to support her in this transition. Everything he said to the veils through which Terri listened sounded like a personal critique leaving her lacking in something. For him it was not because of dissatisfaction; he only felt that a shift had happened and he could no longer play the human part of a 'boyfriend'. With a frustrated shrug, he wondered how anyone would want to continue in a relationship where the other person was not willing.

Maybe tomorrow would bring more peace and understanding.

Chapter Six

The First Meeting

"Courage is the price that life exacts for granting peace."
~Amelia Earhart~

I awoke to another day of churning gray skies, wind and rain. Even though the power in my house had been restored, it was out in much of the surrounding area. Lying in bed, I vividly remembered my visionary dream and the energy that Qua and I seemed to share last evening. Qua's input put a whole new spin on the message being sent through the vision.

The nightstand clock said it was time to stop indulging myself and get up to this new day and all of its possibilities.

First things first, I headed for the bathroom and a warm shower. Stepping out of the bathroom I felt refreshed and ready to see what the day would bring. I went down to the kitchen to prepare my usual light breakfast of fresh fruit and a piece of toast.

Sitting at the table enjoying a fresh cup of coffee, I looked over at the clock to see that it was 9:00 a.m.—late enough to call Qua and resume our conversation as we'd agreed on last night. Picking up the phone I dialed Terri's home number.

"Hello" a groggy female voice answered.

"Terri, this is Danielle. Hope I did not wake you. Is Qua there?"

"Yes, I think so. Do you want to talk to him?" she asked. Not only did she sound sleepy, her voice seemed very sad, so unlike her normal cheery, upbeat personality.

"That would be great. If he is still sleeping, just have him call when he is up and around." I replied, not wanting to press into what sounded like a tense situation.

"Just a minute." I could hear her put down the phone and walk out of the room calling for Qua.

"Hello", Qua's voice came on the phone. He sounded exhausted.

"Hi, this is Danielle. I'm really sorry if I woke you up. Shall I call back?"

"No problem, I'm awake. Just didn't sleep much last night."

I felt a little embarrassed having called in the middle of something that seemed like personal crisis between Qua and Terri, but having made the call I decided to continue so I asked as gently as possible, "I was wondering if you would like to get together sometime soon?"

When he did not answer immediately I continued, "The events of the last couple of days and the effects of my vision are dominating my mind and I would really like to explore all of them with you. I was hoping you could meet me for lunch today, is that possible?"

There was a long pause, then an unsteady, "I could do that. When would you like to meet?"

"Let's make it 12:30 at *Sweet Inspirations*. Do you know where it is?"

"Juelle and Donovan took me there. I'll see you at 12:30," he replied.

"OK, see you then."

Qua's voice sounded removed and unfriendly compared to last night and he seemed to have lost all of his enthusiasm and connection. It left me with serious doubts. I hung up the phone and wondered what I was getting myself into. We hardly knew each other. The events that were bringing us together were not at all logical.

"Not that I am one to follow logic," I thought, "My whole adult life has been one of going in directions based on an inner voice with no clue where it was leading me. Sometimes I think I know, but usually end up some place completely different from what I had figured out." I chuckled at myself thinking, "True to form."

I like to arrive a little early for meetings in order to avoid any anxiety should I run into an unforeseen circumstance. This time was no exception. I was already seated and sipping a lemonade when Qua arrived.

I greeted him with a wave of my hand. Noticing a couple of familiar people entering behind him, I realized that this may have been a poor choice of restaurants since it was a favorite eatery for many of my friends and church members. Hopefully, we would not be interrupted constantly as was often the case in a small town where you are well known. Usually it was fun to visit, but this meeting was going to require focus to get some idea of who and what Qua and I were going to be to one another.

The booth I had chosen allowed for some privacy. Qua slid in sitting directly opposite of me. He was dressed in a silver shirt with large shoulder pads, a gold and indigo lightning bolt pattern splattered across the front. Matching indigo pants, full at the thighs and narrow at the ankle completed his outer-space appearance. Something about his looks and carriage made this type of clothing fit him perfectly. It was hard to tell his exact age. I guessed he was several years younger than I; possibly even as young as his mid thirties. Later I would find out he was older than I thought.

"Hi. Have you been waiting long?" Qua asked

"No. I'm usually a little early so I went ahead and ordered a drink. Before we get started talking, let's take a look at the menu and get our ordering out of the way. The Greek salad is superb and the milk shakes are made the old-fashion way with real ice cream. Very delicious!" I said with a grin.

"Sounds good to me", he smiled back as he closed the menu and laid it aside.

We gave our order to the waitress and settled back looking across the table at each other. There was a long pause as we searched for a way to start this odd meeting.

I was first to break the silence, "I've been thinking about your council, their mission and your search for the meaning within my vision. I believe that you are right, we have spiritual work to do together."

Qua agreed, "How do we open ourselves to explore possibilities?"

Having reached this meeting of the minds, I felt much better. At least we were on the same page. Looking at Qua's face it was clear that he was in no way acting flirtatious but taking the situation seriously. My earlier human concerns about a personal relationship could now be discarded.

"So, why don't we start by exploring our separate visions? Then maybe we can see how they fit together. From a spiritual point of view are you clear about who you are and why you are?" I asked.

"It has been coming to me in pieces throughout my life. My mission has something to do with sound—both through music and toning. Maybe I am supposed to go around the country in my motor home conducting seminars, using my sound equipment, allowing spiritual experiences to be induced. I don't play a musical instrument, however I've been listening to all kinds of music through high-end audio equipment for years. My ear is attuned to the subtleties in sound and I often receive coded information through that modality as well as through words." Qua's face was alight with joy. Sound and music were obviously major components of his life work.

He continued, "I've also felt aligned with the Earth Mission group in Sedona where you and I met a month or so ago."

Realizing I knew almost nothing about him, I asked, "What is your background? What brought you to the Pacific Northwest?"

"I had a successful career in one of the fastest growing computer companies in history with lots of 'goodies'; a substantial income, benefits and reputation. Last year I walked away at my peak earning potential, with no savings or "back-up plan". I sold, or gave away, almost all of my belongings—even my car. I bought an aging motor home, and left California for parts unknown. The only thing driving me to make these decisions was an inner voice and a sense of spiritual destiny calling me into a still mysterious future yearning for some indefinable something."

I listened in amazement. *With very few exceptions, my deeply spiritual friends had an 'alternative' life style—usually self-employed people who lived a fluid outer-world existence. In my experience, people who were at the height of a successful career may dabble in spirituality, but were unwilling to give up a strong personal identity and worldly status. Usually it took some pain and suffering to propel individuals out of a seemingly comfortable life style.*

Qua continued, "I have always had an underlying spiritual focus, even as a small child growing up in a dysfunctional family. But I could never find the answers I was seeking through my exposure to religion. Starting in college I became a seeker through more alternative teachings such as Transcendental Meditation (T.M.). After getting out of graduate school I became a T.M. teacher and practitioner for five years before beginning my engineering career. I studied in Switzerland with Maharishi."

As I listened, I thought how interesting it was that so many people, like Qua, who were drawn to alternative spiritual teachings, had a background of physical and/or emotional abuse as children. Most had always felt that they did not belong in this world or, in many cases, even to the families to which they had been born. They just never quite fit in and often became wanderers. Some used personal will to attempt to prolong their journey pretending to be a 'normal' person in order to fulfill their duty as parents or some other obligations. However, they could never completely ignore that inner voice urging them toward playing some part in a grand scheme that seemed just around the corner of their awareness. I referred to these people as Star Seeds and I considered myself to be one of them.

I asked, "Do you still meditate? Although I've studied many spiritual teachings and have been a spiritual teacher, I've never participated with the T.M. Meditation Technique. I do meditate regularly without any formal training of any kind."

He chuckled. "After fifteen years of meditating, at least twice a day, I found that I could go into that state any time I choose. I could be standing in line at the post office and go into a meditative state. I still sit down and dedicate time to meditation whenever I have an urge, which is pretty frequently." As he spoke, the calmness in his eyes reflected the truth of his statement.

"So, Qua, do you have any ideas as to what we are supposed to do together?"

"I'm not sure. Maybe my music and sound will play a part in your church. It seems very unclear. For one thing, I do not feel comfortable in this geographical area. I've thought that I would end up in Sedona or somewhere in the southwest. My trip up here was mostly to meet Juelle and Donovan after hearing about them from mutual friends. This was going to be a quick visit. As a matter of fact I had trouble connecting with them. Terri and I were headed out of town; miles south of here I decided to make one more attempt at a phone call. They were home; so we turned around and came back to town. I've stayed here much longer than planned."

The waitress appeared and set our food and drinks in front of us.

"Thanks, the salad looks great", I said.

For the first time since Qua arrived I looked around the restaurant. Several people from my church were sitting at a table across from us. As I smiled and made eye contact, they quickly looked away. "How odd", I thought. "I wonder if they were talking about something that's embarrassing. Well, in a town this size, I will probably hear about it sooner or later." I took a drink of my lemonade and turned my attention back to Qua.

He continued between bites of salad, "Terri seems to be ready to settle down in this community. Unknown to me, she rented a house last week while I was in Sedona."

He went on with a worried expression, "I'm clear that I will not be living here with her. We have been traveling together for about six months but our relationship has been in a downward spiral for a while now. Although we're compatible and care about each other, we are not going in the same direction spiritually. It seems to me that we came together at a time when we both needed support to make major transitions leaving our old life. Now we are moving toward a future that does not include one another. It is hard for Terri to understand or accept."

"It seems that even the most graceful ending of intimate relationships are jarring to the system", I said quietly, thinking of Charles and our unfulfilled dreams of spending the rest of our lives together.

"So, where are you planning to stay? Or are you leaving the area soon?" I inquired, hoping he would stick around a while longer.

"I had planned to return to Sedona right away. Having left my career, home, friends and family behind, I have surrendered the next steps in my life to organically sort themselves out. The only reason I came back after this past weekend in Sedona was to finally end things with Terri. There is heartache in the dismantling of my relationship with her, but at the same time, I feel supercharged with divine energy and intimately in communion with my other-dimensional council. After hearing your vision last night, I think I'll stay in the area for another week so that we can explore the possibilities. I'll stay with Terri if she is able to handle it or with Juelle and Donovan. Can you get together with me regularly for this next week?" he asked.

"Yes. I'm past ready to get on with whatever is next and to find out what part we play for each other," I answered. "I've spent the last year watching my life dismantle around me while I felt helpless to stop it. It has been painful even though I knew it was the only choice. I have consciously surrendered into whatever comes even though I have no clear direction to stabilize myself. At some point more visions of the future will reveal themselves."

Not really feeling hungry, I nibbled on my salad. "I know that there is always more to learn. One step prepares us for the next. Right now I would love to experience some sense of destination. Even though I have observed that truly peaceful people are the ones who keep their eyes on the journey instead of constantly being concerned with arriving somewhere. In all honesty, I'm just not there yet—I would love to feel like I have arrived somewhere worthwhile after surrendering so much of what I valued and identified as me."

Qua looked over at me shaking his head up and down in full understanding. We had now touched on something that we clearly had in common—the bridges to our past were all burned and the only direction to move was forward into the mystery of what was to be our destiny.

After lunch we walked out together agreeing that we would meet again tomorrow at my house. It was still completely unclear as to what our Spirits were directing us to do together. The more we learned about one another the more my confusion seemed to increase. We both felt strongly about a solo future of spiritual service—me as a minister, Qua traveling around the country working with groups using sound. The only measureable accomplishment was that I now knew more about Qua's journey and was profoundly moved by his courage and deep spiritual awareness.

Chapter Seven

Rumors Abound

"The mountain of release is such that the
ascent's the most painful at the start;
the more you rise, the milder it will be.
And when the slope feels gentle to the point that
climbing up each rock is effortless
as though you were gliding downstream in a boat,
then you will have arrived where this path ends."

~Dante~

During the next several days Qua and I met regularly attempting to find out what we could do to contribute to one another's mission. While we were growing closer as people, a clear joint vision was not apparent to either of us.

Meanwhile the townspeople would see us in restaurants having, what seemed to be, intimate conversations. I was recognized in the local area because of the church and a few articles that had appeared in the newspaper with my picture.

People who knew of my recent separation from Charles were looking for a reason that this seemingly perfect marriage had ended—another man in the picture was something many people were eager to embrace. The gossip around town had us at the center of a growing story that Qua was the cause of the breakup.

It took a while for me to become aware of the rumors. I started to notice speculative looks directed my way and conversations coming to an abrupt stop when Qua and I were nearby. I told myself it didn't bother me, that I didn't mind the stares and murmurs, the strained smiles and curiosity-laced greetings. Certainly, whatever was being said would pass as quickly as it had begun since it was completely unfounded in truth.

Little did I know that Terri was fueling this gossip by telling all who would listen that Qua had been wooed away from her by me. She evidently believed it herself and was in denial that their relationship had been pretty much over for several months.

Infuriated that another woman was trespassing on what she considered her territory threw her into a tailspin of revenge and retribution. Like many women, Terri saw an intimate partner as protection, while seeing herself as a small, isolated creature, willing to pay any price for someone stronger who would take care of her emotionally and physically. And like so many of her counterparts, she had not yet had the realization that the empty place inside could not be filled by any person. She had lost contact with that part of herself that was whole and loved unconditionally.

I felt confident that many of the people in the community who knew me would not believe the accusations. And, if they had any concerns, they would bring them directly to my attention. They would want to hear my side of the story before forming a judgment. I was soon to find that this was an erroneous assumption on my part.

Feeling confused and disturbed after several days of this bizarre behavior in the community, I felt I needed to talk to someone so I picked up the phone and called a long-time friend, Emily. We had been on a spiritual journey together for a number of years. Emily was considered a spiritual guru with great wisdom. People often sought her out for counseling. I did not think of her as a personal teacher, rather, as a friend and spiritual sister.

"Hello", Emily answered in her soft, melodious voice.

"Hi, Emily, this is Danielle. Do you have a moment to help me out with a little problem?"

"Sure. What's up?" she replied after a moment's hesitation.

"Have you heard the rumors about Qua and me? There seems to be something going around and it is feeling very uncomfortable. I've literally experienced people whispering behind my back!" I exclaimed.

"Well." Emily replied, struggling to get a grip on what to say. "Terri came up to the house for dinner last night. She is very upset and she is convinced that you are the cause of her breakup with Qua."

"My gosh, Emily, that is not at all true! Remember the visionary dream I had last week where Qua played a part? Terri was even there when I told him about it. At the time, he felt it was a coded message that the two of us were supposed to do something together. After he said it, I had to agree, even though it hadn't occurred to me before then. Terri answered the phone the next morning when I called to arrange a meeting with Qua. Anyway, since then we have gotten together several times to explore the possibilities. It's nothing more, nothing less!" My voice was filled with indignation.

"Terri is just trying to figure out what happened. She is devastated over the breakup and is still in love with Qua and thought they would have a long future together," Emily replied.

"Well, certainly we all understand the pain of unfulfilled expectations in relationships. But that does not give her the right to spread rumors. She knows that her relationship with Qua was changing even before they arrived in this area. That has nothing to do with anyone except the two of them. I hope you advised her that I am not the kind of person who would flirt with a man in a committed relationship. Did you suggest that she should talk to me directly rather than continuing on this path?"

"Danielle, Terri feels like a 30 year marriage has just ended and she is still going through the anger. Give her some time. I'm sure she will come around," Emily said in a soothing voice.

"What do you mean by a '30 year marriage'? They were only together for about a year. And, I repeat, I am not in an intimate relationship with Qua! I find your defense of Terri baffling!" I said, struggling to get a grip on myself. I rarely lost my temper because I never wanted to direct anger at others in a personal way. But right now I could feel myself ready to explode with frustration and shocked at what felt like a betrayal by someone I thought was a close friend.

Emily replied, "I really can't talk any more right now. I am about to start a session, so we will have to continue this conversation at another time. I don't think you need to be so upset. If what you say is true, just let Qua work it out with Terri".

"Truthfully, I'm more upset now than when I called. But I guess this will have to wait until you have more time", I replied and we hung up.

The words "if what you say is true" had not been lost on me. Did Emily think the rumors were true? If so, I wondered how two friends who had known each other so well could understand each other's heart so little. I rose to pace off my rising temper and deep sense of grief.

What was happening to the wonderful community of people I thought were my spiritual family and friends? Why would people believe the worst of me after all the church experiences that had brought us so close together? It never stopped amazing me that people could be so quick to believe the worst—it almost seemed like an addiction to the negative. Do people feel better about themselves by believing others to be less—even those they have cared for? Although that seemed to be a popular strategy of the ego, it still hurt when it hit so close to the heart.

Walking across the room, I picked up the phone and dialed Charles at his new apartment.

"Hello, Charles here," his upbeat voice boomed across the line.

"Hi Charles. I need a little guidance. Got a minute?"

"I always have a minute for you, darlin'. What's up?" he replied. There was something about his voice and New York accent that always made me feel that there was not a problem in the world. Of course, I knew it was not really true. But sometimes it felt so good to pretend that I could just turn all my problems over to Charles and he would take care of it for me. With his strong, masculine Telly Savales looks—shaved head, large nose, strong build and fantastic eyes—he would have cast well in a movie as the tough guy who does whatever it takes to get justice. He evoked that 'prince charming on a white horse' kind of false security that felt great right now.

"Have you heard the crazy stories circulating about me?" I asked

He laughed and said, "You know me. No one would dare say anything against you in front of me. What are the rumors?"

"The bottom line is that we broke up because I am with another man." I paused for drama. Then went on, "Supposedly I am in a relationship with Qua. And people believe it—even Emily!"

Chuckling he soothed, "You know better than to let stuff like that hurt you. Just leave it alone. I'll do what I can if I hear anything, but I really don't think people are going to listen to that garbage. Some folks just like to believe the worst in others."

"I know you're right. It just seems to be getting out of hand. Qua's ex-girlfriend, Terri, is telling everyone who will listen totally false stories about us. She seems to have an ever expanding audience.

"Ah, beware of the wrath of a woman scorned! That explains it!" He chuckled again.

"Charles, thanks for listening. You're right. I need to lighten up. I'm not going to hide out or go around defending myself. I'll just make myself available to anyone who wants to ask questions. It is hard to be stabbed in the back if you face your attackers. I suppose Qua needs to get together with Terri to get this cleared up before it gets any more momentum. I'll suggest it to him the next time we talk."

"You're the best. So, how are you doing otherwise?" he asked

"I'm doing alright. Our being apart is still very dreamlike. I keep thinking I'll wake up and everything will be back to the way it was. How about you?"

"I'm fabulous! Life goes on and there is always a gift to be found," he replied with exuberance. "Oops, my other phone is ringing. I'm expecting a call. Can you hold?"

"I'll let you go. Thanks again Charles."

"Alright, darlin'. Hang in there. Just remember, you're the lady who walked on hot coals in her bare feet. What's a little gossip compared to that? I'll see you on Sunday."

Fire Walk Experience

Back in the 1980's I, with a group of spiritual friends, actively participated in human potential seminars and classes led by Tony Robbins. Tony based his teachings on Neuro-Linguistic Programming (NLP) and later became a best-selling author and the inventor of what he refers to as Neuro-Associative Conditioning. In a nutshell, both are very effective methods of altering unconscious programs in the brain.

Tony used his ability to teach people to walk on burning hot coals in their bare feet as a metaphor for breaking through fear and moving beyond the limitations of the mind.

I participated in my first fire walk in one of Tony's early seminars. It was truly amazing and totally beyond the logic of my mind. Truthfully, the only reason I found the courage to actually walk on that twelve foot bed of red hot coals, was that I watched other people doing it without getting hurt and said to myself, "If that person can do it, certainly I'll be able to. And I don't want to embarrass myself by being the only one in our group who chickens out." From my observation of the wide range of age and abilities of the group, walking safely did not seem to require any special physical skills.

I went on to participate in numerous fire-walks culminating with an event on New Year's Eve at Tony's castle in Del Mar, north of San Diego. This event was to be the longest, hottest fire-walk any of us had ever done, thirty feet in length using Mesquite wood which allowed for extremely hot coals. As I arrived with all my friends there was excitement pulsing through the air. We spent only about 30 minutes preparing with visualizations and mantras then walked out to what seemed like a blazing inferno.

As I neared the front of the line where Tony stood making sure each person was prepared for the walk, my fear began to grow. The heat coming off the coals was so intense that my plastic covered name tag began to shrivel.

When it was my turn, I looked at Tony with fear obvious in my voice, "I'm not ready. I really don't think I can do this."

"Go. You're ready." he assured me.

"I really don't think I am."

"Yes, you are. You can do this." He pronounced with absolute certainty in his voice.

My mind was in a jumble of thoughts, "How can I do something that I don't completely believe. On the other hand, I've done it before and today others have already gone ahead of me. If they could do it, can't I. I'm not sure with my doubts. Don't I need to be 100% sure to be successful?"

Something suddenly clicked from inside and I made the decision to go. All uncertainty moved below the surface and I just walked—successfully reaching the end without any pain or burns; even the long silk pants I wore survived unscathed.

This experience put a serious crack in my belief that I needed to be fully in control of my thoughts in order to successfully create my desired outcome. It also made it abundantly clear that we are using only a small portion of our body's capacity. After the fire-walk, I would contemplate possibilities like walking on water, astral travel or manifesting out of thin air. Many things now seemed possible, even for an average person.

Reflecting back on all the crazy rumors floating around I wondered why people want to believe the worst in others and so often inflict pain by expecting people to live up to their expectations. They sit around and complain, or gossip, repeatedly about the way another individual acts, or does not act, and it's all based on personal opinion and desire. Individuals in the congregation wanted Charles and me to stay married and felt they had a right to criticize us for not continuing to give them what they wanted.

I've observed that everyone does what makes sense to them according to their own values, awareness and beliefs—period! Each person looks out at life through a set of filters that create the world around them. I've watched two people standing side by side looking at the same thing and see it in a completely different way.

I reflected on what happens to children as they grow into their own and break away from controlling parents or marriages where one in the couple dominates the other. The suppressed party either gets angry and leaves or stays and looses a part of him or herself in the process. Ultimately, no one will follow another person without becoming resentful.

I thought about my friend, Kim, who had a grown daughter with children. The daughter expected Kim to be the type of person who relocated to be near the grandchildren so she could babysit and bake cookies. Kim had a choice to make; either attempt to satisfy her daughter's values or honor her own truth. In this case, she knew that she would only feel resentment by giving into the daughter's demands since it was not in her nature to dedicate a large portion of her life to a grown daughter or grandchildren. It made more sense in Kim's reality to keep her heart open and live by her own standards. She honored her own path too much to sacrifice it out of some false sense of obligation or an attempt to prove to her daughter that she is loved.

———————————

Overcoming, or bypassing, fear by taking authentic action in spite of it had become a way of life for me. Charles' advice was correct. I would not let a few false rumors and the expectations of others govern my life. Silly judgments were a small thing compared to a life lived to its fullest by taking risks, living on the edge and following my own inner guidance.

Chapter Eight

A Woman Scorned

"If you bring forth what is within you,
what you bring forth will save you.
If you do not bring forth what is within you,
what you do not bring forth will destroy you."
—*as attributed to Jesus Christ in The Gospel of Thomas*

Qua arrived at my house the next afternoon for our fifth meeting in as many days. High in my thoughts was to discuss his relationship with Terri. We went into the living room and sat cross-legged facing each other on the couch in front of a newly started fire.

"Before we continue our investigation about our joint mission, I want to talk about something that has really been troubling me for the past couple of days." I went on to tell him about the rumors and the reactions of those I had spoken to as well as the stories Terri had been spreading around.

Qua sat quietly listening until I finished. After a moment's reflection, he said, "Wow. I had no idea this was happening. I've been staying at Terri's house. All of my worldly possessions are there commingled with hers. She has been understandably a little upset, but usually acts cheerful and friendly. Truthfully, I have been avoiding talking about the separation in any detail.

I know there are things to work out, but I was positive she was in agreement that the relationship is over and it is time to move on. She knows I am leaving for Sedona in a few days and have no plans to come back."

With a look of disbelief, I said, "She may be pretending to agree to the separation. But according to my friend, Emily, she is very upset and looking for a way to get back together with you. She is stirring up a hornets' nest in town. I think you better have a serious talk with her as soon as possible. I will be happy to call her myself, but I think first you need to clear things up."

Qua's face was showing signs of real discomfort. He obviously would rather not deal with Terri. "I've been very clear. I'm not sure what else I can say to her."

It was obvious that Terri acted one way in front of Qua and quite differently when he was not around. However, I did not want to play the part of the 'other woman' or continue to find myself in the middle of a sticky personal relationship that really had so little to do with me.

The problem was—how to get out of it while continuing to leave the options open with Qua. This whole situation was confirming my desire to stay away from intimate relationships. They are so susceptible to misunderstandings, jealousy and manipulation.

Another part of me completely understood Terri's fear and desperation. It was common for women in the church to seek my council when a relationship broke up, in those times when they felt alone and unloved, when they had lost contact with that part of themselves that stands for strength and had mistakenly placed it in the hands of a man, those times when they needed to be reminded that in God's eyes we are all completely loved and protected. Spiritual integrity is the true source of our strength and safety.

"I know this is uncomfortable to talk about with me or to confront with Terri. However, I can't see any way around it. You will most likely have to be brutally frank with her and come up with a clear exit strategy to end the relationship cleanly," I suggested. "It seems that in your attempt to soften the blow, she has been left with the impression that there is a way to repair the relationship. Don't be deceived, Terri is not accepting whatever you have told her so far. The truth is that her main focus is finding a way to get back together and gathering as much support around town as possible. I definitely am not willing to start defending myself from these stories or counter attack Terri. The only strategy that makes sense to me is to talk to her directly. It is always best to be direct and honest even if it hurts at the time."

"You are probably right. I'll call her right now to see if we can get together. May I use your phone?"

"Sure. Why don't you use the one in the kitchen where you can have some privacy? I need to run out to the barn to feed the cats and I'll be right back."

Qua watched Danielle walk away, thinking, "I'm not liking this. What started out a few days ago as exciting new possibilities to explore is becoming an emotional mess. From a spiritual perspective this is quite simple, Danielle and I are assigned to explore ways to join in service of our Divine Mission. The assignment to be with Terri is complete. Neither have anything to do with the other. I'm finding it difficult to decipher the source or reason for all this confusion and continued upset."

"For two cents I'd rent a car and head south right now. This whole situation reminds my emotional body too much of the relationship with my mother and sister and their constant bickering and even physical fights."

Sitting in the barn petting the cats as they ate, I remembered a talk I attended a few years ago given by a medical doctor. I can't remember his name. His personal theory on the primal fears of men and women starts with the life experience of the sperm and the egg. He asked us to imagine what it was like to be a sperm—travelling up the canal with millions of other sperm in a competition to reach the egg. In order to be successful, the sperm must work with others, accept death and be out to win.

In the meantime, the egg is sitting all alone in a protected environment. Along comes a few sperm. As soon as they get close, the egg reaches out, consumes one or more and they merge into one.

The theory is that the primal fear of the male is being consumed by the female and loosing himself. The primal fear of the female is being alone.

Over the years I have asked numerous people (both male and female) if this seemed true and overwhelmingly people agreed that it had some validity.

Remembering that story, my compassion for Terri increased and I sent a prayer for peace, well-being and love. If nothing else, I felt better.

———————————

With me out of the house, Qua picked up the phone and dialed Terri's number. She answered on the second ring.

"Hello", she answered in a shaky voice.

"Hi, Terri, how are you doing? You don't sound like you're doing well."

"Oh no, I'm fine. I'm glad you called. I was wondering if you were coming home for dinner?" she asked cheerfully, quickly getting a grip on her mood.

She sensed that Qua was more comfortable when she was upbeat.

"Actually, I was calling to see if we could get together and talk. Dinner will be fine, but don't go to any trouble. We could go out somewhere if you would rather."

"No. Let's eat at home. I already bought food and was planning to cook anyway", she said a bit too quickly.

The use of the word 'home' put up red flags in Qua's mind. He was tempted to insist that they go out somewhere more neutral but did not want to press the subject. Maybe the privacy would be better for their discussion anyway.

Qua agreed to arrive around six o'clock and hung up the phone with a sigh of resignation over the inevitable storm that was brewing. Why, he wondered yet again, would anyone want to stay in a relationship when the other person was no longer interested. It is so demeaning to everyone involved. But he also knew that many of the emotions that seem common to women were completely unknown to him . . . and to most men, he supposed.

When I walked back in the house from feeding the animals, I found Qua sitting at the kitchen table with a perplexed look on his face.

"What's up?" I asked.

"We'll have to postpone our meeting today. You were right. Terri has not accepted the change in our relationship. I guess the next thing on my agenda is to get this cleared up and make some definitive plans for Terri and me to go our separate ways. I'll have to take off and will call you in the morning to re-schedule."

Looking at him with concern I said, "I wish there was something I could do or say to make this easier."

"Thanks. It is what it is. Hopefully enough time has now passed that she is ready to accept the inevitable outcome."

Qua arrived at Terri's house to find a romantic setting complete with candles, soft music and the delicious aroma of roasted chicken. Terri was dressed in a seductive outfit and had gone to a lot of trouble creating an atmosphere of intimacy. Her objective for the evening was apparent.

Looking around Qua shifted uncomfortably. Tension leapt into the air around them. "Terri, I think we need to have a totally honest talk. This is not going to work for us. I am not here for a romantic evening. I'm sorry if you misunderstood when I agreed to come."

"Oh, don't worry. You know me. I love to create beautiful environments and delicious food", she said in an overly bright voice. "This is a celebration of our new home. I'm not expecting you to jump in bed with me, if that is what you were thinking."

Ignoring her last comment, Qua said, "Terri, this is not my home. It is your home. I'm leaving next week and do not plan to come back. As far as I am concerned all that is left to do is to work out the details of dividing our stuff."

"What about Danielle?" she asked with tears trapped in her throat.

"Danielle and I are exploring a spiritual assignment. She has nothing to do with why you and I are no longer together," Qua answered calmly.

"You've been seen together all over town, making me look like a complete idiot! And don't tell me about 'spiritual assignment' whatever that means! I'm sick of all your spiritual jargon and metaphysical philosophy. Get real. What we have is an of-this-world relationship," she exclaimed and then burst into tears.

Qua waited a beat, in shock over her outburst. He knew Terri wasn't realistic about their relationship, but had not realized that she was carrying all of this pent-up emotion and resentment. Terri had always appeared to have a lightness of being and joy that permeated her life and their months of traveling together. For a while Qua mistakenly thought that they were sharing the same spiritual path. "And now," he thought, "it appears that she was just pretending to go along with me in order to stay in the relationship."

As calmly and quietly as he could manage he said, "I think I'd better leave. We can talk again tomorrow after you have had a chance to accept that we must go our separate ways. It was never my intention to hurt you. I am truly grateful for the time we have spent together. It really is not personal. I'm just being pulled in another direction by my Spirit."

Terri pressed her fingers to her eyes, fighting for control of her emotions. This was real and it hurt—to her it was very personal.

Slowly and deliberately she drew in a deep breath, looked at Qua through tear-filled eyes and asked, "We meant nothing to you?"

Qua looked down, feeling helpless to ease her pain. What was there to say when they were coming from such a different spiritual realities. How could he explain when she was only interested in getting what she thought she needed from him?

He turned and walked toward the door. "I'll call you tomorrow when you have had a chance to sort this out for yourself. That's all I know to do right now."

———————

As Terri heard his car pull away, she sat down at the beautifully set table feeling paralyzed. The candle glowing on the table and the smell of roasted chicken in the oven seemed to mock her for her foolish hopes of a life with Qua. Her face filled with grief at the thought that all the dreams she had sought to fulfill were now forever lost because of another woman.

Chapter Nine

Divine Marriage

"Yesterday is but a dream, tomorrow is but a vision,
But today well lived makes every yesterday a dream of happiness
And every tomorrow a vision of hope.
Look well, therefore to this day."
—Ancient Sanskrit proverb

The phone was ringing as I returned home the next morning after a quick dash out for a cappuccino at the local drive-through. It was Qua calling from a motel in town.

"Hi, just wanted to fill you in on my emotional evening with Terri."

He highlighted the conversation from the previous evening and his growing concern that Terri was very confused about his intentions and feelings.

After listening carefully, I said, "I've noticed that men and women are usually viewing relationships from a very different place. It becomes apparent in situations like this. Our expectations and needs are held right under the surface and these hidden agendas bubble up when the relationship ends or changes form. If both parties involved are not willing, or able, to tell the truth about their feelings, it can become very messy indeed!"

Qua pondered this for a moment. "I'm not sure what to do next. The inner voice of my Spiritual Council is clearly leading me away from Terri and has been for quite some time now. I guess I'll give her another call to see if I can get her to understand. I want to support her. I just don't know how. I'm leaving in a couple of days and want this cleared up."

"Where are you staying? Are you still at Terri's?"

"No. I left last night and checked into a motel", he replied

"You are welcome to sleep on my couch; it opens into a bed." My mind immediately questioned the wisdom of this offer. If people found out Qua stayed overnight at my house it would most certainly fuel the rumors. On the other hand, my life was dedicated to following my inner voice, not the dictates of others.

"That would be a welcome alternative! I am nearly out of cash. Let's see. I am supposed to check out by eleven. Would it work for you if I came over around four o'clock? Then we can spend more time sorting through our connection."

"Works for me." After a moment's pause, I asked, "Qua, when you call Terri why don't you see if the she would meet with both of us before you leave town. Then we could talk it all out in one session. What do you think?"

"Maybe," he reluctantly replied. "She may not want to meet with the two of us together."

"I'm sure she won't want to. But for me it is time to be firm and insist on getting all of our feelings out in the open and stop getting everyone in town involved."

"I know what you mean. I'll let you know how it goes when I come over this afternoon." Qua seemed miserable at the idea of being in a room with Terri and me. I knew he wished there was some way to avoid the whole mess but I could see no way around confronting the situation head on.

"OK. See you around four o'clock. I'll put something together for dinner", I hung up the phone with a sigh.

I immediately began to worry about where this whole thing was leading. In our talks over the past week we had been viewing life through a bigger picture; attempting to decipher the messages being received through dreams and inner voices. Looking at possible ways we could serve humanity together through joining forces and sharing our individual spiritual journey and visions for the future. All of it felt totally on-purpose and empowering. In the excitement of the journey together, our bodies would sometimes feel surges of male/female chemistry. This was experienced in the natural flow of being together, however we did not empower these impulses with action. Both of us felt that we were together for a higher purpose yet to be revealed and did not want physical intimacy to detour us off course.

I thought this latest chain of events felt like a very small story; one that was uncomfortable and totally off-purpose. "Who cares about rumors, lies and needy women? Maybe my visionary dream was not about Qua personally and is not leading to a blend of our missions. Before the dream I was fully prepared and quite sure that I would be alone for the rest of my life working as a minister and spiritual teacher. Qua and I had no interest in each other beyond respect and spiritual connection."

The voice in me returned with vengeance asking the inevitable questions. Was this temptation to join forces with a man an unconscious fear of being on my own? Was I moving forward in exploring a relationship with Qua because of an inner calling, or was I reacting to hidden motivations resulting from deep fears. After all, I really didn't know Qua very well and all indications were that his relationship with Terri was filled with distortions. This was too vulnerable a time in my life to take a side-trip into some personal drama that would take me off course and dim my ability to listen to inner guidance for direction. The more time I spent with Qua, the more he seemed to dominate my life. Realizing where my mind was taking me, I cautiously withdrew from these dangerous thoughts that were leading me down a path I was determined to avoid.

I felt a new resolve to step back and take a truthful look at my motives. First, I needed to distance myself from Qua, while maintaining an open channel to any communications about him from my Spirit. My plan was to go only as far with this adventure as felt safe. No more getting in the middle and letting myself get pulled into someone else's personal drama.

That evening as Qua entered my old fashioned country kitchen and asked if he could help set the table for dinner, I felt my body tense. My face remained passive while my thoughts screamed, "I do not want any man knowing his way around my kitchen. Please God; I just want to live my life in service without participating in the confusion and distortions of close-in, personal relationships!"

I answered, "No. It is all under control. Just sit down and make yourself comfortable. Dinner will be ready in about ten minutes."

Qua felt the tension in the air and a distance from me that had not been there until now. "Are you alright?" he asked

"I'm fine." I replied stiffly.

"You seem less calm and centered than usual. Did something happen since we talked this morning?"

"I'm just tired of all of the drama. It seems so petty and unnecessary. Did you get a chance to talk to Terri?" I replied with an edge in my voice.

With confusion on his face, Qua said, "I talked to her briefly today. The three of us are scheduled to meet for dinner tomorrow evening. What do you think? You don't have to go. I can go alone."

"I'm sorry. Of course I'll go. I really do want to get this cleared up as soon as possible. I'm just finding it hard to be put in a position of defending myself against all these lies and misunderstandings. Especially in a community of people I thought was my spiritual family. I never would have believed that this scenario could happen to this group—and with me right in the middle of it all. We have bonded so deeply on so many occasions. I feel angry, confused and saddened."

Qua was at a loss to know what to say or do to alleviate my discomfort. He agreed that he would rather have the whole situation just go away so that we could go back to spending our time in spiritual pursuits.

After dinner we retired to the living room and attempted to continue sharing visions and insights. However, the problems with Terri seemed to repeatedly slip back into the conversation. I would attempt to resolve it by understanding the deep psychological reasons this was happening, while Qua would talk about it as destiny and spiritual assignment. I was quite sure that Terri would not appreciate or understand Qua's "metaphysical" explanations, since she was identifying herself as a woman scorned and in need of healing. Qua did not know how, nor have any interest in, lowering his frequency to accommodate Terri's identification with pain and suffering. He felt she needed to look from a higher perspective.

In the end, the conversation kept going in circles and getting us nowhere. The only chance of resolution would have to wait until the next night when we were together with Terri.

"Let's go out and rent a video." I suggested.

"Good idea. It is nearly nine o'clock. Is there a video store nearby?"

"There is a small store with video rentals right down the street. I noticed that they had the 1984 movie, '*Starman*'. I love that movie and you remind me of the main character."

"Really? I've never seen it", Qua replied.

"You are kidding! It is such a great movie! Let's go right now and rent it!"

We stood and eagerly walked toward the back of the house in the mud room to get coats and shoes for the short drive. We were feeling relieved to move out of the bleak mood that had been sitting between us the whole evening.

With popcorn sitting in a large bowl on the coffee table and wrapped snuggly in a warm blanket, we sat close together as the movie began. The introductory credits were still being shown, when there was a knock on the door.

"Gosh. It's almost ten o'clock. I wonder who that could be." I exclaimed as I paused the video, stood up and walked over the answer the door.

Looking through the glass, I saw Michaela standing on the porch and suddenly remembered her call last week asking if she could spend the night. I opened the door with a smile and welcome.

"Michaela! Hi! I totally forgot that you were coming. What a pleasant surprise! Come on in. Have you met Qua?"

Looking a little taken back by Qua's presence, Michaela replied, "No, I have not. Good to meet you, Qua." Turning back to me, she asked, "Is it still alright for me to stay here tonight?"

"Of course. I apologize for my lapse in memory. I've gone through a stressful few days and lost track of time. We made popcorn and were sitting down to watch the video, 'Starman'. Your timing is perfect. Have you seen it?"

"Yes, years ago. I would love to watch it again."

"Great. Just drop your stuff right where it is and come make yourself comfortable. I'll get another cup of tea."

As Michaela and Qua got better acquainted, I went into the kitchen. When I returned everyone settled in to begin the movie. The story concerns an alien who landed and took the shape of a young man who had recently died leaving behind a grieving widow. From the beginning I was struck by the similarity between Qua and the main character played by Jeff Bridges. Like the character, Qua possesses qualities of innocence, charm and other worldliness and a certain graceful, awkwardness in his body. At times he moves like a dancer and has very quick reflexes. At other times he seems uncertain about how his body works. Often he seems in tune with others and possesses profound wisdom; and within moments he appears completely disconnected from worldly reality.

Toward the end of the movie, I began to think about where everyone would sleep that night. I had two choices—either bunk in with Michaela in my bedroom upstairs or with Qua on the hide-a-bed couch. My logical, mental body told me to sleep with Michaela. After all, should anyone find out I had slept in the same bed with Qua; it would make it appear as if the rumors were true. However, the message from my inner voice vibrated with a knowing that I was to stay beside Qua for yet unknown reasons.

The movie ended leaving all three of us feeling deeply connected in a state of peace and grace. It awoke a memory held in our bodies of another more evolved world; a world that was just a breath away. For several minutes we sat quietly enjoying the serenity of being in each other's company. I took note of the feeling that Michaela, Qua and I knew each other from some other reality.

I finally broke the silence. "Was that wonderful or what. Michaela, I'm so glad you were here. For some reason, it feels important that we are all together in this time at this place. We may never know exactly why."

"I agree. I'm not sure what just happened, but I know it was good", Michaela answered.

"It is now nearly midnight", I pointed out with a yawn. "Guess we had better get some sleep. Michaela, you can stay upstairs in my room and I'll crash down here on the couch."

"OK. I'll see you in the morning." Michaela said as she picked up her belongings and headed upstairs leaving Qua and I alone.

Surprisingly the idea of sleeping in the same bed was not uncomfortable for either of us. After brushing our teeth and turning off the lights, we lay down on our backs holding hands and immediately fell into a deep sleep.

We spent the night in a vivid visionary dream visiting another dimension. Wearing golden robes and accompanied by the sounds of distant water and nearby bells we led a throng of iridescent Beings into a massive temple. Supported by our soul family and surrounded by song and toning, we participated, communicating telepathically, in a ceremony of merging—a divine marriage. As the ceremony progressed it seemed as though our bodies disintegrated into sparkling molecules, then reformed so that we were somehow touching inside—mind, heart and Spirit. This pageantry of unconditional Love was an incredible experience—magical and profound. Despite a sense of mystery, the place was very familiar to both of us. It felt like our sacred home. After the ceremony, we stood holding hands looking into the eyes of our spiritual family; immersed in gratitude for the blessings being bestowed upon us.

———————————

As my mind arose from the depths of my dream state, I opened my eyes, and turning my head, I looked into Qua's remarkable hazel eyes. We were lying on our backs, holding hands with our faces turned toward each other and had awakened at precisely the same time. It was as if we had just brushed our teeth and gone to bed a moment ago.

Ordinary words could not convey the depth of our feelings. Talking at the same time, working within the limitations of language, we attempted to describe our profound dream. It was only then that we realized, to our utter amazement, that both of us, simultaneously, had lived a vivid, sacred experience. It would have been an astounding occurrence for either one of us individually. Yet, we had experienced the exact same vision—one of being merged together in an elaborate ceremony leaving our consciousness quickened. Usually we were both exceptionally light sleepers making us further stunned that the entire night had passed in the blink of an eye.

Looking up we saw Michaela coming down the stairs with her overnight bag in hand.

"Good morning. Are you two already awake? I'm running late. Thanks for the great evening. I'll see you next time." She said as she dashed by us and out the door.

We watched as she exited, unable to say anything in our present state-of-mind beyond a mumbled, "Goodbye."

We now knew, without a doubt, that we had been brought together for a divine purpose. The closeness between us was almost visible; the connection was ancient. Overnight we went from experiencing strong resistance to any kind of personal relationship to no longer being able to imagine our lives without being together.

We accepted that we were not only ready for these strange events surrounding us, we were meant for them and they for us. Whatever bound us together gave us no choice but to continue down a joined path.

Without words, from a place deep inside, we knew that whatever our unified role was, we would fulfill it.

Chapter Ten

Dinner for Three

"People turn to God when their foundations are shaking,
only to discover it is God who's shaking them.
Faith involves a basic trust in the universe—
That everything is for our highest good."
~by Dan Millman

Dazed and filled with a feeling of bliss, I wandered through my day with new aliveness, forgetting why I'd entered a room, unable to focus my thoughts on anything but my new relationship with Qua. How astonishing that a man I barely knew a week ago had become the center of my universe. We found ourselves looking at each other's smallest gestures with fascination—the way he stuck his chin out when he was concentrating—my habit of leaning my head to the right and lowering my eyes when I was confused or uncertain—his ironic humor, often with a play-on-words, that filled me with laughter. There was something so familiar and endearing about every personal characteristic. It was if we had always been missing an essential part of ourselves and it was now appearing in the body of another person.

Occasionally, I could hear my mind shouting in the background of my consciousness, "What are you doing. It was just a dream. Snap out of it!

Remember yesterday when you were ready to do a grand exit if the situation did not shift very soon. What about the fact that you will be going your separate ways tomorrow when Qua takes off for Sedona with no plans to return. You are entering into a dangerous state of affairs, for both of you. You must not latch onto this guy, acting like he is your reason to exist."

And yet, it felt right & real. Although I knew that these were all legitimate concerns on some level, they just did not matter anymore. The impulse to move forward with Qua was more powerful than my desire to humanly maintain control of my destiny. My only choice was to give myself over to this fate. Some sacred event had been orchestrated last night bringing us together in a way that was too profound to be denied.

Having already freed himself of most of his worldly ties, Qua was more at peace with these changes. What was being brought into his life did not seem to be more questions, but answers; making sense out of the process he had started a couple of years before when he began to feel urges, beyond all logic, to leave his career against the advice of everyone around him. He had grown adept at following his inner guidance without knowing where it was leading, "living in the mystery".

———————

The rain had stopped and the evening was clear and cold as Qua and I walked huddled together toward the restaurant door. We could see that Terri had already been seated. As we entered, she looked up. Her sense of betrayal showed clearly on her face.

"Hi", Terri called out raising her hand in a greeting. Her eyes were trained on Qua, ignoring me completely.

"Hi", I responded with a smile, recognizing the animosity in Terri's body language and wanting to neutralize it with a reminder of our previous relationship of friendship.

Terri gave me a wary look full of suspicion and frustration as Qua helped me into the seat beside her, then sat down across from the two of us. My heart went out to her knowing how much pain she must be experiencing. At the same time it was difficult to pull out of the blissful energy Qua and I had been feeling all day.

Bodies shifted uncomfortably around the table as we began studying the menu as if fascinated by its contents. The air around us was pulsing with unease. Finally Qua looked up and suggested that we just order a pizza and some salad to share. Everyone agreed, relieved to have the decision made. We sat nervously trying to find a way to start the conversation. The waitress walked up to take our order, breaking the deafening silence.

"We'll share the vegetable pizza. Hold the mushrooms and onions. And we'll have a large salad to share. I'll take a Coke", Qua said

I smiled at the waitress. "I'll have lemonade."

"Just water for me", Terri added with downcast eyes and a weak voice.

Looking over at Terri, Qua was feeling guilty about his own happiness and not sure where to begin. "Terri, we really just want to have you understand. I'm not leaving you for Danielle. The relationship between you and I has been that of friends for a long time now."

"Maybe for you, but not for me! I left my whole life behind to go with you. We were planning to be together traveling around and finding a place to settle down. What happened to those promises? You start a relationship with someone else and you expect me to just smile and wish you well. You expect me to believe it has nothing to do with our breakup." Her face was filled with grief, as if she knew that whatever she was seeking was already lost.

"Terri, we have different missions. We started out supporting each other in moving out of our old lives. We each knew we needed to change. It has been great and I really care deeply for you, but we do not have a future together as a couple. We have been growing apart spiritually and at some level both of us knew that this separation was inevitable. We have been skirting around these issues for a while now. I was hoping we could make this transition without embittered feelings. Both Danielle and I want to support you in starting a new phase of your life. It seems you have found a home and community that has welcomed you."

Terri sat paralyzed for a moment. Her throat caught. She did not want to appear weak knowing Qua preferred strong women. She was not giving up without a fight. She hoped that what she saw as Qua's infatuation with Danielle would end as quickly as it began. In time, Qua would realize that it was a mistake to walk away from all the dreams they had shared and she would be waiting to take him back.

Our food began to arrive, giving all of us a little time to ease the emotional tension. Eyes downcast, we began eating without tasting. After a few bites, I glanced up at Qua with a soft look of love and support. He smiled and continued scooping up bites of salad.

"So, Qua, what are your plans. Are you going back to Sedona?" Terri asked breaking the silence in a bright, vivacious voice. *Just beneath her brightness she was feeling barely in control, an earthquake of emotion was locked inside her body.*

"I'm planning to leave tomorrow, unless you would like to have me get my stuff out of your house before I leave." he answered.

"No. You can leave it there. I have plenty of room. Are you driving the motor home?" *Terri definitely wanted to keep their material stuff intermingled so that the break was not complete.*

"No, I think we should sell it. We could both use the money. Maybe you could call that consignment lot along the freeway to see if they could take it."

"Sure. When are you planning to come back?" *Terri was feeling some relief having the conversation turned to subjects that did not include Danielle.*

"I have no definite plans right now. I know I have to get my things out of your house and tie up loose ends. We can be in touch by telephone", Qua answered as he tore off one end of his straw and turned his attention toward me. With a playful smile, he blew the paper at me. I laughed in response.

Suddenly the tension around the table was off the scale with intensity. Terri seethed as she watched us. *This was the kind of intimate interaction that was reserved for her only a few weeks ago. How could this be happening? Some part of her had hoped that the relationship between Qua and Danielle was just a passing thing, with no lasting depth. But she knew that Qua was not playful and relaxed with people who were not extremely close to him.* Terri gave us a look that could only be described as murderous.

The look on Terri's face truly made me flinch. As I replayed what had just happened in my mind, I knew what had set Terri into a tailspin. Qua, on the other hand, felt the shift but was completely puzzled as to what caused it.

Terri's face turned mutinous as she said, "I really have to go now. Thanks for dinner". *Her heart was pounding and her body trembling as she quickly stood up, only half hearing our response, and walked out the door into the cold night. She immediately felt the void Qua left, as if a piece of her life had been taken away. She took a deep breath, but it wasn't slow and it wasn't easy. Her chest heaved with emotion as sobs shook her body. Under the tears were thoughts of retribution but she knew it was her anger speaking.*

A wave of anxiety ran through Qua and I as we watched her petite form retreat into the night. Tears pressed against my eyes. Qua sat astounded at the depth of Terri's emotions and her lack of willingness to let go of their relationship. In his mind, they had gone over all of it not once, but several times. Neither Qua nor I could think of a solution to regain peace and understanding between the three of us. There was nothing to do right now.

I felt compassion for Terri's deep yearning for a committed partner. What she didn't yet understand was that Qua could not fulfill that desire for her. So many times I've seen women who want more than their partner is able to give, and yet, they cling in hopes the feelings will change. In the end their neediness drives a deeper wedge between themselves and their desired outcome.

I was aware that ultimately no one wants to fulfill the perceived needs of another. We are all on a unique journey of self discovery and evolution. When we are evolving together, it feels like an upward spiral. When we are clinging or judging one another, relationships go into a downward spiral of pain. To me, it's that simple.

"I guess we are going to have to wait this one out", I suggested, my expression softening. Inside, there was a feeling of foreboding that went through me, the kind of tingling of the skin and tightening of the throat that foretold events to come.

Chapter Eleven

Separation

"The universe if full of magical things
patiently waiting for our wits to grow sharper."
~Eden Phillpotts~

Early the next morning Qua prepared to leave for his previously scheduled trip to Sedona. He had rented a car to make the drive. It felt wrenching to be parting, but we knew it was what was being asked of us individually and as partners.

As we walked toward Qua's rental car with a suitcase between us, I experienced a sense of grief, almost like a part of me was dying. I couldn't help but express this in words, "We have come together without any of the accoutrements of a courtship and yet I feel as if we were spiritually married in our dream-state. We are not lovers and we don't even know what we are supposed to do together. Yet, we are meant to be together. Everything tells me that. I know that there is a purpose bigger than either of us alone. I just don't have any idea what it is. Even if it turns out that I never see you again, you will always be a part of me."

"I'm feeling the same way. I'm clear that we are being asked to be together. We both know that when Spirit speaks, it does not tell us where we are being led—only what to do next on the journey." Qua said, taking my hands in his strong warm grasp.

"You are right. I just wish there was something I could focus on to stabilize all of this craziness. It would be great if I could just jump in the car and take off with you right now!"

"Why don't you?"

I looked at him for a moment visualizing what it would be like to go back to the red rocks of Sedona and relax into the sacred energy of the place.

"No. As tempting as it is, we both know that I'm staying here. The church is closing today. I'm going over there with a truck to load up the last of the boxes. A small group of people, including Terri, have been packing up everything. After last night, I'm not looking forward to spending time with her. But it will be good to get closure on the church and then wait to see what is next. The council still has not determined if we will be focused on moving the church to Olympia or finding a larger location locally. Oh, I just remembered, I'll be in Los Angeles this coming weekend to attend an event and to visit my daughter, Alex. She is attending Occidental College. Why don't you drive over from Sedona and meet us at the Ramada Inn in Santa Monica on Saturday? I already booked a room for Saturday and Sunday night."

"Sure. I can do that. In fact, I'd like to do that. It's a form of contact that I think we need right now. Guess I'd better take off. I'll call you from the road this evening". We hugged and stepped apart.

As Qua backed out the driveway, I felt unwanted tears fill my eyes and mark my cheeks. I swallowed trying to dislodge the lump forming in my throat.

I stood watching Qua disappear from sight; my thoughts struggled between hopefulness and despair. Finally I slowly turned toward the house. In spite of my unhappiness at Qua's departure, I had an inner sense of optimism and surrender assuring me that everything was on a path of evolution toward the highest potential. There was no doubt; I was being asked . . . no, ordered, to give myself over to destiny.

"This is so bizarre!" I said to the wind and the trees. They seemed to nod in agreement.

Meanwhile, Qua's mind was in overdrive:

This whole series of events was not at all what he had planned, even for him with his freedom and willingness to follow Spirit, this was pretty strange.

"Maybe," he thought, "I just need to let it go for the time being"

Qua popped in one of his favorite traveling CDs—sat back and focused on the pleasure of being on the road again. As the miles flowed beneath him his mind wandered back into memories of his life.

Qua's family had been walking in the park . . . a rare family excursion for his parents, his younger sister and himself. They walked, not as a family who cared for one another, but almost in single file. Qua brought up the rear—odd for a child of only four years old. He recalled the sun slanting down as if spotlighting his parents and sister. In that moment it was completely clear to his youthful mind and body that these people were not capable of providing support of any type, be it spiritual, emotional or even logical social support. Qua knew he would be fed and clothed to the best of their ability but beyond that he was on his own. More than that, he was the family caretaker subject only to spiritual inner guidance

With no parental guidance Qua lived as if he was an orphan, free to follow his own path; the path lit by inner knowing. It was only his physical and mental strength and his connection to other worlds that allowed him to survive and function.

Qua knew, from an early age, that he was a step away from others. Before the age of twelve he had visions that explained the workings of the universe. When he tried to ask or to share these experiences, the adults in his life responded, "Shhh, we don't talk about those things," or, "That's nice dear. Now go outside and play with the other kids."

Qua's companions were all too often frustration and loneliness.

As a young adult the feeling of separation from others was still there but less significant. By then he had accepted and trusted his own spiritual awareness and begun to search the world for spiritual traditions. After graduate school at the University of Illinois, Qua spent five years learning, practicing and teaching Transcendental Meditation (TM). Eventually he began a career in the computer industry, but underlying all of life was his fascination with spirituality and his part in the greater scheme to come.

―――――――

Returning from memories, Qua's mind shifted to the near present. He'd known for over a year that he was to step into the void. That was the reasoning behind shedding material belongings and accepting a RV life style. He knew that before him was a major turning point, although he had no idea what that would look like.

The past week's experiences and the two amazingly vivid visionary dreams . . . all fit with his previous spiritual patterns. Since his pre-teen years he'd received coded information—words and visions—that sent him into an altered state where further information was downloaded. Often Qua would find himself in a catatonic state for ten minutes, or more, before returning to this reality to find he was altered in profound ways. These things he accepted as a part of who he was and is today. Still, he'd never before had a shared vision with another human being, nor had he ever had such a clear knowing that he was to intimately share life's journey with another person.

Qua drove further south aware that the climate and landscape was shifting dramatically . . . a metaphor, perhaps, for what was to come.

One of the things that confused Qua was that he had no feeling of connection to any church—to any organized religion. Even as that thought went through his mind he suddenly remembered a profound experience from the past.

––––––––––––

While still working in the computer industry in southern California, Qua attended a counseling session utilizing a technique called Radiance Breathing. It was designed to reveal inner emotional blocks. He was in a dimly lit room lying quite comfortably on the floor ready to begin a guided exercise. The Radiance therapist placed pillows strategically beneath his arms explaining that blocks were often released in the form of rage. The pillows would allow him to pound the floor without bodily damage.

Qua was asked to relax and coached in the deep radiance breathing technique. He followed the guidance he was given, overriding his instinctive desire to go into a meditative state.

Without warning Qua's breathing shifted, becoming quick and shallow. The floor no longer supported his body; he was floating, weightless, not upward, but downward. The sensation of floating and falling continued for some time. He was aware of the therapist's gentle voice as a distant background sound similar to falling rain. Finally, his downward spiral ended. Qua was lying on the forest floor surrounded by vivid orange and red autumn leaves. A tiny creek gurgled softly nearby; a few colorful leaves floating in its quiet pools. Sunlight slipped through branches overhead dappled the scene.

Instantly his awareness shifted. He was one of the leaves lying on his back and looking up through the branches of the trees toward the light while gently floating on the meandering water. It was surreal—like a watery song or a Monet painting.

Supported by the softness of the clear water, he came to rest. A shaft of light seemed to focus between the branches overhead aiming directly at him.

Qua looked up, through the light to discover he was standing at the foot of the crucifixion of Christ!

His body shivered. His heart pounded, drowning out all thought, all sound. He experienced existing as the essence of Self overwhelmed by the passion of the Christ.

In that cathartic moment, Qua felt the complete essence and depth of the Christ consciousness. The true and complete significance of the crucifixion was infused into him as he stared up with tears in his eyes.

Vaguely, and from a great distance, came the voice of the therapist saying,

"It's OK to pound the pillows," while she layered blankets over Qua's trembling body.

He began the long journey back into a waking state gradually becoming aware of the concerned therapist watching over him. Another thirty minutes passed before his shaking body quieted and he was able to speak.

Qua reflected, "Was this a gift from God filled with Divine Grace." To this day it is difficult for him to think or speak of this experience without a wave of deep emotion as he reconnects with the Christ energy of Divine Love.

———————

Meanwhile, life in Washington State went on for me. Unaware of Qua's thoughts, I entered the house determined to see only the optimistic side of this situation, but as I moved to tidy up the room I was aware of an emptiness . . . a feeling that something was missing. It was as if I had forgotten to wear a coat when it was cold outside or forgotten that I had to do something very important. This unsettled feeling had me walking in circles accomplishing little.

Early that evening Qua called, "Hi, I just stopped in Ashland, Oregon for dinner. How has your day been?"

In that moment, it was absolutely clear that Qua was the thing missing.

"I'm so glad to hear you voice and feel your energy. I've felt so odd since you left this morning. For the first time in my life being with another person seems to make me feel more complete than being alone. In the past it has always taken energy to be with other people, even those I love. I guess because I worry about fulfilling their needs and desires. When I'm alone, there is a sense of peace and rejuvenation; it's a time when I can move in my own rhythm, listen to my councils and enjoy the moment. It's weird and a little embarrassing to admit, but I am feeling incomplete without you here."

"That's exactly how I am feeling. A few minutes ago as I exited the freeway. Suddenly I became aware of tremendous spiritual energies running through me, far beyond what is normal, and then I began channeling. The information from my council was clear and strong that we are to be together. It's spiritual destiny at play. Any doubt I had is now completely gone. My personality feels like turning around and coming back, however I know that this trip to Sedona is part of the plan. We'll be together in three days when we meet in Los Angeles and I'm certain the next step will be revealed. In the meantime, I'll call regularly so we can stay connected."

The calm sound of his voice was the tonic that stitched the frazzled quilt of my fragmented world together. "I'm so relieved that I am not alone in this. If you were not having the same experiences, this would be hard to take or even trust. It is such a radical shift in a short period of time. I'm not sure anyone could understand if I tried to explain it."

Focusing on the new information Qua had given me, I asked, "Do you channel regularly?"

"No, it is highly unusual for me. At least not in this way where I feel a presence come through me and speak. It was a phenomenal experience."

"Qua, I'm not sure where all of this is leading us. All I know is that we are meant to work together. Everything tells me that. The future is a total mystery. Usually I have the illusion that I know where my life is taking me. Not this time!"

"I'll see you again soon."

"OK. Drive safely. Be sure to pull over if you start channeling again," I said with a smile.

Qua laughed, "We'll still be with each other even without being together physically. Our bond is not dependent on the physical."

"Of course, I know that on most levels. It is all just moving so fast that it's a challenge for my mind to quiet down. I'm feeling bewildered, excited and apprehensive all at the same time."

"I can totally relate. I'll call tonight after I stop somewhere," he reassured me and hung up.

———————————

Over the next couple of days it became obvious that Terri was on the war-path. Whenever I saw acquaintances and friends in town I sensed undercurrents, some subtle and some overt. At times my heart felt like it was going to shatter.

It was especially vivid when a group of us, including Charles, met to pack up stuff at the church. Terri had been there earlier but left when she was told that I would be coming by. It was obvious by the stiff posturing of several people that they were judging me harshly. No one commented or asked questions. Anything I thought to say would sound critical of Terri thereby adding energy to the distortions. The only person who seemed at peace with the whole situation was Charles. The reason was simple—Charles truly knew me and did not question my motives or values as anything but Soul-driven.

I noticed that when a person feels attacked, the ego wants to counter by getting others to collude with their point-of-view, creating at least two groups of opposing positions. I felt confident, in this situation, that I could convince most, if not all of the people in the community, to see things from my point-of-view and to judge Terri for her behavior. However, I knew that this strategy would create even more turmoil and pain and would only serve the dictates of my ego while diminishing the voice of my Spirit. The price was too high!

It was apparent to me that wars in families, communities and nations are caused by egoic, fear-based attacks and counter-attacks ending in amazing losses for everyone involved. Fighting to be "right" and make someone else "wrong" never ends well.

I wondered again how such a thing could be happening. It was beyond my ability to understand how a person like Terri could come to town and disrupt the community and my world to this extent. The only thing I could think to do was to pray and look for the gift being offered; knowing that nothing ever happens that does not have a spiritual agenda for those with eyes to see it.

I began to feel optimistic when it occurred to me that having the community breaking away was allowing me to easily move into whatever assignment my Spirit had for me and Qua. I no longer felt overly attached to continuing the church or even living in the area. At the same time, I was willing to stay and heal these distortional energies if Spirit so desired. I felt detached from any outcome, allowing my heart to be open and tuned to the voice of Divinity as it directed me into the mystery of what was to be my future.

Life is like a treasure map—always leading to the glorious prize of Self Actualization.

Chapter Twelve

Meeting in Los Angeles

"The Dance will take on a new tempo
As the harmony that emanates from within
sets the pace for other kinds of experience."
~Oneness, by rasha~

In the face of all the drama, I went into isolation for a couple of days. It felt like I was losing myself, feeling increasingly more disconnected from the things in my life that only last week gave me a sense of purpose and relationship. The unique attributes that identified me as a separate personality, with individual preferences, passions, dislikes, talents and direction; all had shifted. Bottom line, I was experiencing a profound identity crisis. It left me feeling weak, as if the always dynamic life force within me was dying. Looking back I could see that this had been happening for about a year but now it was reaching a tipping point.

Usually, when I felt my life spinning out of control, I would turn to my close friends and find solace as well as insight to move toward clarity. This time, there was not a single person who could even begin to understand let alone offer assistance. To the rest of the world, I had just ended a loving marriage for no apparent reason. No one could relate to the speed at which my world had turned and the relationship with Qua had begun. Marriage to Charles seemed a long time in the past, even though it had only been just over a month since our separation.

Finally, it was Friday morning and my interior turmoil was set aside by action. I was disembarking from my early flight to Los Angeles. I was scheduled to meet Qua the next day after having completed an intense spiritual event with a small group of people with whom I had shared numerous gatherings over the years. This group was made up of hand-picked individuals who were willing to go to the outer edges of reality in search of spiritual awakening. The group leader, Tim, was and is an amazing man who, among others, assisted me to better understand some of the structures of the Universe in which we live and vividly experience Divinity in all things. Tim was the kind of guy who could lead you unscathed through the flames in a burning building or, with equal brilliance and precision, through the distortions of your unconscious mind.

Not long after this particular session began, Tim and I realized we were experiencing a lesson in cosmic humor. Neither of us knew how it began, only that a mere glance at one another brought forth hilarious, unstoppable laughter. We found ourselves bending over holding our stomachs, tears rolling from our eyes. We were experiencing the entire world and everyone in it as a huge cosmic joke. It allowed my body to release pent up tension, fear and confusion. As it turned out, this was a perfect preparation for what was about to happen.

After leaving the event on Saturday around noon, I drove over to my daughter's dorm room at Occidental College and knocked on the door. I was suffering from a severe migraine headache which I mostly attributed to all that laughter, intensity and lack of sleep the night before.

"Come on in, its open." came a shout from within.

Drawing a deep breath, I opened the door to a sea of color that reflected Alex's joyful, youthful energy. Alex was the epitome of the goddess—with her tall, curvaceous body, long thick hair, beautiful green eyes and full lips.

When Alex saw me she dashed into my arms with a jubilant laugh, "Hey, Mama. How ya' doing?"

"It's great to see you. I've missed you. But, as pleased as I am to see you, I have to admit I have a killer headache."

"Oh Mama, is it one of your migraines? Let me give you a massage. It will just take a minute to set up my table."

"Honey, that would be so wonderful."

Alex had been touching people with her magical hands since early childhood. She was born with the gift to nurture and heal. Her abilities were always a blessing to me when I suffered one of my chronic headaches that seemed to come right before a major spiritual breakthrough. I had found no healer in my life that could alleviate the pain as did Alex. From the moment she was born, I knew that this child was a gift to the world and that we had spent many joyous lifetimes together.

With relief at the prospect, I slowly removed my clothes and climbed on the table. As Alex massaged my body, I could feel the tension being released and replaced by a sense of relaxation that had eluded me for weeks. Some deep and permanent shift was happening in my consciousness. Something that I did not yet understand but knew, beyond a doubt, that divine forces were actively involved.

When the massage was over, a feeling of contentment flowed through me along with the wish for a nice long nap. Time, however, would not permit that as we were already late in leaving for the hotel in Santa Monica where we were to meet with Qua.

As we drove along the crowded freeways between Pasadena and Santa Monica, I attempted to explain to Alex my relationship with Qua. I did not go into very much detail. After all, like so many others, for Alex the separation from her specially selected father had just happened. While she was a very allowing and understanding person, I did not want to cause her undue concern nor did I know how to accurately explain it.

I pondered how difficult it was to tell anyone what was happening without having them think that Qua and I were experiencing romance as portrayed in books and movies. Most romantic fantasies are based on 'need fulfillment'. Our relationship was, and still is, rooted purely on a sacred knowing beyond reason. Neither Qua nor I felt a need to be in an intimate relationship and did not see one another as fitting a picture of the perfect woman or man. Our love did not stem from sexual attraction, a need for companionship, money or worldly status. We just knew that we were profoundly assigned. That is not to say that the traditional romantic ingredients were completely missing; they just were not the motivating force behind our being together.

As we pulled into a parking space at the hotel, I felt a quickening in anticipation of being in the physical presence of Qua once again. Entering the front doors, I spotted him sitting in the lobby and quickly walked over.

"Sorry we are late. Have you been waiting long?"

"Actually I was thinking of getting in my car and driving back to Sedona. I feel very uncomfortable in the frequency of Los Angeles. It feels strange; too many people, cars and noise." His tone was distant, without emotion. His eyes were cool as he regarded me.

I stood stunned for a moment. A wave of anxiety ran through me. Was everything we had experienced unraveling before my eyes. Had I been in some delusional state of mind? I looked up into his eyes and, for a terrible moment of paranoia, I felt I didn't really know this man at all. Maybe he wasn't the one sent to be with me; maybe he was just playing a game to see where it led and was ready to bail the first time it felt too uncomfortable.

"Are you serious? You were about to leave?" I asked, unwanted tears pressing against my eyes.

"I'm just very uneasy here. Let's check in and go up to the room where we will be out of all this weird energy."

Suddenly I remembered that Alex was standing with us. Turning toward her I made hasty introductions. After expressing the automatic pleasantries, we began walking in uncomfortable silence to check in and find our room. Once inside, Alex excused herself saying she wanted to go for a walk.

"So, what is going on?"

"I'm just feeling out of my element in this town. I've been waiting for over an hour, not knowing where you were or when, even if, you would show up. I left Sedona where I felt at peace only to arrive in this superficial world. It just got to me. I'm very uncomfortable here," he repeated.

"I really do apologize for being so late. Do you still want to leave and make other plans to get together at some point in the future? Or, are you having new thoughts about our connection?"

"I've been looking forward to being back together. I guess the waiting downstairs and the traffic getting here threw me off balance. Let's just start over," he said quietly and smiled.

I let out a long breath, still reeling from his reactions and at the same time relieved that our connection was not broken before it even had a chance to be fully explored.

"I'm for starting over. This whole sequence of events has been very unsettling for the mind. Let's go find Alex and get some food. I have not eaten much of anything all day. How about you?"

He smiled, "Sounds good to me. Do you have a place in mind?"

"There's a restaurant within easy walking distance. It has outside seating that overlooks the park and ocean beyond."

We walked companionably through the hotel and into the snack bar where Alex was sitting sipping a Mocha and chatting merrily to the person next to her. She looked up with a big smile, noting that the tension seemed to have dissolved between her mom and this new friend. Relieved from the lack of stress, Alex took a moment to observe Qua as they walked toward her. She liked what she saw but would never have guessed he would be a companion for her mom.

Qua was so different in every way from the men previously in my life. For one thing, he seemed a lot younger than the worldly types I generally chose.

Qua had a youthfulness that made him seem closer to Alex's age. Plus he was tall, dark and handsome in a quiet way. In the past I had chosen older men with powerful personalities so unlike this gentle almost monk-like person.

Alex was watching, intrigued, as the two of us approached. She smiled murmuring, "One thing about my mom, she is never boring!"

Part Two

~ Vishara ~

Chapter Thirteen

Walk-in Experience

"We are on the verge of the new age, a whole new world.
Mankind's consciousness, our mutual awareness,
is going to make a quantum leap.
Everything will change. You will never be the same.
All this will happen just as soon as you're ready."
~Das Energi, by Paul Williams~

As dusk eased into night we fell right into easy conversation and laughter with Alex in the mix. The evening passed in warmth and the pleasure of the three of us being together. The hotel room had two queen beds, Alex and I taking one and Qua the other. As the lights turned off I was left with my thoughts and emotions; I struggled to get a grip on reality. Being bone tired didn't seem to matter; I could not get to sleep.

I knew, without doubt, that there was order in the world; a method to the Universe. In my heart, I knew that people are born with spiritual DNA; a set of signals leading us all through life on a very specific course. I also knew that these signals are often muffled in layers and layers of pain, fear and self-judgment. Yet, these invisible strands of suffering could be undone; I had both assisted and watched people unravel them very quickly after

115

an experience of profound self realization. The key is in recognizing the difference between your True Self, or Soul, and the mind-created personal identity. Finding the shut off valve for the insanely loud egoic mind allows the still, quiet inner voice—the voice of the Soul—to be heard.

Finally I fell into a sleep of pure exhaustion. Sometime later I awoke with a jolt, the feel of a cold hand squeezing my heart. My dream was reliving Qua's earlier behavior and it touched a deeply painful place inside me. With a determined focus on my true identity and a prayer for release, I began slowly to feel the energies of separation and fear dissolve. Gradually, I slipped into light slumber and as my True Self returned I was able to spend the remainder of the night in a deep refreshing sleep.

As if by unspoken agreement, we awoke late in the morning and drove to a superb little restaurant along the beach front for brunch. Alex was joining a friend from college and driving back to campus that afternoon. Again, with Alex's cheerful energy present, the flow of the conversation was light, interesting and fun. By the time brunch was over and Alex said her goodbyes and drove away with her friend, Qua and I were somewhat more comfortable in each other's physical presence although weariness remained under the surface.

Hand-in-hand we walked to the car relishing the smell of the ocean air and enjoying the gentle breezes as they murmured through the tall palms lining the street. While enjoying the moment and the presence of Qua, I wondered what I was, truthfully, expecting from this relationship. There were no promises, no plans, no soft words of love and desire. Was that what I wanted? I'd had that with Charles, and it was not enough to keep us together. What weakness was it in me that craved those fairytale promises and words?

By the time we reached the hotel I felt worn out. My logical mind thought it was from a lack of deep sleep and my frustrated attempts to figure out my life and inner guidance. I suggested that we take a nap. It was highly unusual for me to sleep during the day, but nothing else seemed more appealing right at that moment. It was almost as if my body had taken control and demanded something for itself. The freshly made bed looked so inviting. I slid into its luxurious comfort and fell into an immediate deep slumber.

Walk-in Experience

Waking from a sleep that had taken me into other realms, I gradually became aware of warmth and the fact that my body was lying on something soft and smooth. I was curled in a fetal position with the soft weight of a blanket covering me with protection. I slowly opened my eyes seeing a muted unrecognizable room. I was unable to remember any recent events with any clarity.

Qua, sitting on the other bed reading, was aware of a shift in energy within the room and circling my body with womb-like warmth. He took a quick peek in my direction.

Seeing my open eyes, he smiled, and asked, "How did you sleep?"

Hearing him through a mist, I forced a mumbled, "Fine. Have I been asleep long? I feel pretty out of it; very strange and empty inside." A segment of my brain noticed how muted my voice sounded.

Qua, aware that something unique was occurring slid from the bed and took the two steps across to where I lay in my befuddled state. He wrapped me in his arms with quiet strength and soothing comfort. With a fuzzy laugh, I turned my face against the curve of his shoulder.

I remained passively at Qua's side, slowly becoming aware of a phenomenal shift taking place; I felt totally helpless and unable to control my thoughts and movements. I hadn't the will to do or say anything. My body no longer belonged to me. It felt like I existed within a thick fluid in some neutral space just outside of Earth's reality.

Neither Qua nor I were clear as to what was occurring, but Qua, with his unique spiritual perspectives, knew that he must continue to hold the body of Danielle with confidence that the life force, weak as it was, would survive the experience through the wisdom of Spirit.

My only recourse was to surrender to whatever was occurring in and around me. I was faintly aware that my body, my life force, was maintaining itself; at the core of my body, the heart continued to pump blood, albeit at a very slow pace. My breathing was barely perceptible. My human mind, usually so very active, was extremely quiet—a mere whisper to be noted without concern or emotion. The experience of my unique personality was no longer vivid in my awareness; my physical, emotional and mental bodies were completely neutralized. I had no preferences—no opinions—no desires—and no worries. It was as if I were floating in the womb of Spirit. My personal identification was being altered forever.

And so it was that at approximately 10:00 p.m. on a Sunday, the soul essence of Danielle exited the body and a new soul to later be named, Vishara, was born.

Qua recognized that the body he held no longer harbored the soul of Danielle. He became concerned and watchful, wondering if he was still assigned to whomever had just arrived in this dimension. What little remained of my mental awareness passively wondered if this was some sort of reaction to the intense workshop I had just completed. Even with my nap, I still felt sleep deprived. Within my mental apathy I wondered if this unearthly experience might pass by tomorrow.

———————

The next morning arrived with no change in my status. The original soul, Danielle's soul, was leaving and someone else was clearly in the process of birthing. I still felt that empty, mentally vague, floating stillness inside. It did not seem that I even needed to breathe to maintain life. As to what was happening or why—those questions wandered passively through my head but there was no energy to try to answer them. There was very little energy to think about or remember anything.

A 'walk-in' or 'soul rotation' experience is as dramatic as the birth of a newborn baby. The phenomenon, like channeling, is a natural expression of the body even though it is seen, by some, as strange. For many it is beyond strange; it is unbelievable.

A couple of months earlier, while living in the RV, Qua had a similar walk-in experience. He was left transformed; a completely different person. He was still in the process of learning what it means to be a human in the late 20th century. His fluid lifestyle had allowed for an easy integration and acceptance of his radical shift in identity by most of those around him.

Looking back, Danielle—now Vishara—realized that the departure of the original soul was much like that of a human death. The life force within her body had been weakening for some time. She had recognized the lack of physical energy and the mind apathy over the past several months and wondered if she were going to die soon; both fearing and embracing the possibility.

I was scheduled to fly back to the Pacific Northwest that day. However, it became immediately clear that whoever "I" was in my body was not very functional yet. I could not seem to focus my thoughts, make decisions or easily complete straightforward tasks such as brushing my teeth, taking a shower or getting dressed. Each action took an inordinate amount of concentration to remember, even the routine and simple everyday activities. My perception of reality, physically and emotionally, was completely different.

The phone rang while Qua was in the shower and I automatically picked it up.

"Hello." I mumbled.

"Is Qua with you?" a voice asked testily.

It took several moments of focused attention for me to access the memory of this voice and some of the circumstances around it. I asked, "Is this Terri?"

"Yes. Is Qua there?"

"He is in the shower. Want me to have him call you?"

"No! How dare you speak to me in that soft lethargic tone of voice! You are staying in a hotel room with my boyfriend and have the audacity to pretend nothing is happening?" she asked with venom in her voice, "Who do you think you are?"

"Terri, I . . . ."

Angrily, Terri interrupted with, "Are you about to attempt to convince me that you two are staying in the same hotel room, but not having an affair! That this is some kind of spiritual assignment! Give me a break", she almost shouted.

With an inward sigh and forcing myself to focus, I replied, "If you want to talk to Qua, he just turned the shower off."

"Put him on right now!"

I handed the phone through the door to Qua and could half hear him as he attempted to calm the raging storm coming through the phone from Washington State. I was oddly unaffected, emotionally, by the drama. It was almost as if I did not even know Terri or have any opinion about her. There were vague memories and images, but they seemed meaningless.

Qua stepped out of the bathroom with a sad, frustrated look on his face.

He remained silent and seemed to be studying me. "So, what do you want to do? Are you flying back to Washington or staying with me on my drive up the coast to San Jose?"

"I honestly don't have a preference nor do I feel any answer from within. It's strange that I am so disconnected and don't even care. I know I should, but the truth is I don't. What do you think?"

Qua decided for us both; I would stay with him and drive up the coast giving me time to stabilized.

Qua wasn't particularly happy about his current situation. His personality would prefer distancing himself from the whole drama of Terri's anger and, as evidenced by the recent phone call, it continued to follow him. After all, he was not even sure he was still assigned to be with this new soul. Maybe now that Danielle had left, their time together was ending. However, when he looked inside for direction, he clearly knew that they were to stay together—at least for now.

As it turned out, our journey together over the next few days started an intense integration of the two of us and the birth of a new soul into the body of Danielle while her soul ascended into other dimensions of reality.

It was becoming apparent that the fluctuation of deep feelings interspersed with mental confusion that Danielle and Qua experienced from the moment of their first meeting, was preparation for their coming together in preparation for my arrival and the bonding of Qua and I as we embraced our divine relationship.

Chapter Fourteen

Body Integration

"Awakened, you perceive the potential that
has not yet taken form.
You see the ideas of eternity, and from among them
you choose the ones you will help into time.
Your perception itself draws their fields of
potential into tangibility."
~Starseed, The Third Millennium, by Ken Carey~

Driving north along the shore of the ocean on Highway 101, I found myself in a magical new world. My sensory perceptions; smell, taste, touch and even color were sharper and more dramatically alive. It was as if Qua and I were separate from the rest of the world in some rarified bubble. I was having difficulty remembering my life before this new reality overtook me.

From my altered, or perhaps refined, perception all this seemed entirely normal. Although I was still disoriented from the soul rotation, I was tuned in to subtle energies. I could see crystalline light particles with iridescent colors floating on delicate streams of energy everywhere I looked.

The ocean was the color of sapphire with light particles that took the shape of jeweled clusters glittering on the water. The soothing roar of the surf was a backdrop for the squawking seagulls overhead with their white bodies, the sun flashing golden light off of their spread wings. The smell of the salty air was so fresh and delicious that it seemed eatable. It felt good to be in a body and to feel alive once more, especially in this vivid, pulsing reality.

For a while after the walk-in experience, I was not sure that I would ever feel anything again or, for that matter, care about anything again. I did not yet fully understand that the original soul essence, Danielle, no longer inhabited my body. Even though I knew there was a radical change, accepting it as a permanent change had not yet occurred to me. I was very aware that Qua exerted a magnetic pull. Every other point of reference in my life was gone; except for Qua. He was the only person in the world that seemed real and relatable. I wanted to tell him everything and find out everything about him. I wanted to share our private and spiritual lives in great detail, somehow knowing that we could then merge the past into the present, leaving no part of ourselves that was separate, one from another. Although my memories of my past were vague, as I talked, they would spring back as if being unlocked from the cells of my body. I experienced being present behind the stories. It was as if I were telling events from someone else's life, someone that I knew intimately.

Looking toward Qua, I asked, "Tell me more about your sacred journey."

"I guess I'll start from the childhood this body experienced. I attended a Presbyterian Church with my family, but I could never find the answers I was seeking through my exposure to religion. In junior high school I started reading about, and becoming fascinated with, utopian ideals. In college I became a seeker through more alternative teachings. I explored the mystical side of various philosophies.

Later, I began Transcendental Meditation (TM). After only a few months, this practice brought great peace and emotional balance to me and to my social life. My grades rose dramatically, allowing me easy entry into graduate school in engineering at the University of Illinois.

I felt so strongly about the benefits the meditation technique held for people of all walks of life, that I enrolled in the teacher training program held in Europe. I left for the training the day my graduate thesis was successfully completed. After six months of training, I returning to the Midwest, and spent the next year as a full time teacher in the TM organization. Then, to my delight, I was able to return to Switzerland for advanced training from Maharishi. The many years and depth of meditation prepared this body's nervous system for the extraordinary transformations in consciousness that have occurred since then. I feel very blessed and privileged to have been able to instruct almost 300 people over a four year period. I have lived a life that allowed me to immerse myself fully in the wisdom and pure meditation experience."

As Qua talked, memories from my previous life continued to come back into my awareness and, at the same time, it felt like I was able to live his experiences with him or at least fully integrate the essence of them.

We talked on and on, sharing detailed stories about the people we knew, the experiences our bodies had lived through and the insights we had gained. At one point Qua asked me to tell him about my channeling experience.

After a moment's hesitation, I began accessing the memories. "Channeling was the first truly unexpected spiritual experience that happened through this body. Prior to channeling, I had always believed that thoughts create reality and I am in control of my thoughts, therefore, I can create my own reality. It made sense to me, so I spent time doing lots of affirmations, creating treasure maps, visualizing, forcing myself to think positive thoughts and making myself wrong whenever I did not get what I thought I wanted; not that it did not work sometimes—just not all the time. In 1990, I was attending yet another human potential event when suddenly I began speaking in tongue. It just started spewing out of my voice box without my conscious will or understanding. The people around me were amazed and excited. The facilitator of the event began to encourage me to continue. By the way, this was not a seminar to learn to channel—it just happened!

At the first break, I jumped in my car, abandoning the rest of the day's activities and headed home—wanting to get as far away as possible. Even though I had been in the audience watching and listening to channels on a number of occasions, it had never occurred to me that I would become one. I felt out-of-control and concerned over what was accessing me since it wasn't something I knowingly invited, in addition, I did not understand the gibberish that was coming in.

By early that evening, the energy in my body built to such an intense level that I no longer felt I had any choice but to let it speak through me again. I called my mentor and friend, Dorothy, and asked for some help. She dropped everything and rushed over to assist me in preparing my body and surrendering into the mystery of it and the knowing that it was mine to do.

Within a couple of days, the Beings were speaking in the English language although they still occasionally spoke in tongue. In those first years, I was completely unaware of what they were saying as they spoke through me. However, they were very much around all of the time in my daily life giving me insights and assisting me with my spiritual evolution. The one who speaks now is called Zantron.

After I began channeling, I realized that I had not fully believed that this phenomenon was truly happening to people. Deep in the back of my mind I felt it was an individual's higher Self and was made available because that person was uncomfortable or shy about speaking divine truths. Boy was I wrong!

These days, when I channel, although I am still pretty vague about what is said, memories will come back occasionally. It is sort of like when you wake up in the morning and remember a dream; then it seems to fade away if you don't focus on it immediately. That's how it is for me."

———————————

And so it went as we talked and drove on for hours; pulling threads of energy from our past and weaving it into a new tapestry that became one combined fabric. The only solid place in the universe was the two of us. Who I was before last evening had dissolved. As Qua told his stories, his calm melodious voice was slowly stitching my fragmented reality together into something, or someone, new. We were like a single entity, poised on the edge of Earth's reality.

Looking over at me Qua asked, "Do you think your name is still Danielle?"

"No, I don't. I love the name Danielle, yet the frequency is not reflective of who I am in this body." Pausing for a moment I said, "I think the new name will come to me very soon."

I continued, "It is really odd how attached people have become to their birth name. They act as if God spoke from the heavens, "Your name is Danielle—or whatever!" Therefore, it is your "real" name. Yet, women usually change their name when they marry.

To me, a name is both personal and impactful. Each word spoken has a harmonic signature. When you repeatedly hear certain harmonics directed at your personal identity, it has a powerful affect. Because having a name that more accurately matches an individual's higher frequency is deeply empowering, I was anxious to learn my new spiritual signature.

Settling back in my seat, I closed my eyes and drifted off into a half sleep; I was still aware of being in the car, but deeply relaxed. After a short time my new name became apparent to me. The harmonic, or sound, of the name 'Vishara' most closely matched my Spirit's identity.

Slowly I opened my eyes and became fully aware of the world around me.

Turning to Qua I said, "My name just came to me from my inner knowing. It is Vishara."

He smiled, "Yes, Vishara feels like a perfect sound for who you are. Vishara it is!"

I added, "That feels so right" and sat back in a very relaxed state with a smile on my face.

"Is it so right that you'll never feel the urge to respond to the name "Danielle" again or fail to answer when I call you 'Vishara'?" Qua teased.

Grinning, I replied, "I may be in Danielle's body with her cellular memories, but the soul now occupying this body is new—it is me, Vishara. I do have a vague curiosity as to how receptive other people will be to this profound shift. I'm quite different than Danielle. When people think that they know you, it is common to stop observing what is true in the moment; instead, friends, co-workers and family will hold you to their preconceived perceptions of the past. I'm sure you have experienced that. What was the name given to the original inhabitant of your body?"

"Anthony with the nickname of Tony," Qua responded. "It is fascinating to discover who has trouble accepting change, even in others. Some very casual friends of mine had the biggest reactions, even refusing to call me by my new name. While others that I expected to have a problem with my shift in consciousness, were very allowing and supportive."

As I thought back, I remembered that a few friends could not accept the channeled entities coming through me. The only thing they could see was the body and not the shift in energy and frequency. Amazingly, my two daughters could easily see that it was not their mom speaking. Shannon, who was in her early twenties at the time, had a strong reaction at first. She asked Zantron, with tears in her eyes, "Where is my Mom?" I don't remember anyone telling me his response, however, after that she seemed to settle into the process.

The sky had deepened from blue to light indigo as day eased into dusk. A full moon hovered just above the horizon. We realized that, with the exception of two gas stops, we had not pulled over to eat, drink or even stretch since leaving Santa Monica that morning.

As we made our way up the curvy road with cliffs falling off to the rocky shore below, we noticed a sign saying that we were five miles from Big Sur.

"We better find a place to stay for the night in Big Sur. It's getting late and I'm not sure how far we will have to go to reach the next town," Qua commented.

"You're right. Given how long we've been on the road, I am amazed that I don't feel tired or hungry; but it may hit us all at once. I've only been to Big Sur a couple of times and, as I remember, most of the town is tucked away in the forest. I stayed in a cabin off the main road but would have no idea how to find it again."

As we entered the town, it was as I remembered with very few shops, restaurants or motels in evidence. We were almost through the town when we spotted a vacancy sign up ahead.

"Let's check this out. As long as it is clean, I'm O.K. with it. What do you think?" Qua asked.

Within a few minutes, we had checked in and settled in a rustic little room toward the back, away from most of the street noise. Qua put a tape into our recorder and music filtered through the room.

The bed looked so inviting that soon we were lying down face to face, looking into each other's eyes with mounting intensity. Qua reached toward me, his touch was curious but gentle and, whether or not he intended it to be, erotic. Our light conversation flowed gently along as the energy of music permeated our bodies and a heat began to shimmer like magic around us. The air appeared to be golden and rich with energy. Softly, I put my hand on his chest, feeling the beat of his heart under my palm. We moved together and shared our first tender kiss.

The surge of desire came instantly and was irresistible. An unbroken river of energy swirled around us. As we joined together, I felt as though we were absorbing each other through the very cells of our bodies. The merging inside erased all separation and opened me to my True Identity in some remarkable way. As we abandoned ourselves to the flood of sensation, waves of happiness washed through me, completing the joining and leaving my body suspended in quiet harmony with this new soul.

In this sacred reality we could actually see through the veils to watch a celestial light show, with a multitude of extraordinary lights shooting through the air. They appeared similar to the Northern Lights, only with sharper edges and strange, as well as familiar, shapes revealing themselves and then vanishing as quickly as they came. The air was pulsing with energy, displaying itself in different hues and colors. It was apparent to me that I was glimpsing the merging of Qua's other dimensional council (the Royal Light Command) with my councils. In this place, time seemed irrelevant.

As we began emerging from the transcendent nebulous space we had occupied, our vision returned to a more solid world, although it still appeared quite ethereal. It was hard to assimilate what had just happened, but I knew that our joining had fully awakened my soul into this body.

I whispered, "That was bliss!"

Qua smiled and gently cradled me as we became aware once more of the music filling the room and the night sky with countless diamond bright stars peaking, with sparkling eyes, through the tall fir trees outside the window. Together, we drifted into quiet sleep.

Chapter Fifteen

Unconditional Love

"Always act as if the future of the Universe
depended on what you did,
while laughing at yourself for thinking
that whatever you do makes any difference."
~Buddhist teaching~

Upon awakening a few hours later, we felt a little lightheaded and remembered that we had not eaten all day.

Qua turned to look at me on his way to take a shower and said, "It's already 10:00 p.m. Let's see if we can find some food somewhere around here. It might be challenging at this time of night."

I smiled affirming my agreement, "It's hard to think about going out after what we experienced earlier, but you're right, our bodies are past needing some fuel."

We had been so possessed with energy since leaving Santa Monica in the morning that we did not seem to need sleep or food at all. However, the realities of our bodies were proving otherwise.

Throwing on our discarded clothes after quick showers we headed out. We discovered that the restaurants in the sleepy town of Big Sur were locked up tight. The only place that we could find open was a local bar. Even assuming they served something other than drinks, this was definitely going to present a problem given my taste in food. Being a vegetarian and eating almost exclusively organic, it could be difficult to find anything I wanted in most all eating establishments, let alone a bar.

We walked in, sat down and asked if they served meals.

"Yes, here is a menu. Pretty much any of it will be available except for baked potatoes," replied a pleasant young man behind the bar.

"Could I get you a drink?"

"I'll take a Coke or Pepsi." Qua requested

"Do you have lemonade?" I asked

"Sorry, no lemonade; the only non-alcoholic drinks are soft drinks."

"Then I'll have a Root Beer."

We settled back to peruse the menu. Suddenly, we both felt extremely hungry. Most things looked tasty to me, even foods I normally never ate. Finally, we settled on a hamburger and fries for Qua and a vegetarian burger and salad for me.

When the food arrived we dug in with gusto. It tasted so wonderful, making us realize the length of our day and how famished we truly were. Clearly, we'd been operating on an energy level far different from the norm. After eating about half of what was served, our body energy had been sufficiently supported and we were ready to go back to the motel for a good night's sleep, not to mention a much needed chance to integrate what was happening.

The next morning, the distant traffic noise outside our window broke into my dreams. As I awoke slowly to the serene light filtering through the room, I lifted my eyes to Qua's face. *"Real"*, I thought. *"I wasn't dreaming."* Joy filled me so completely that I wished only to burst with the energy of it. I studied Qua as he slept; full, romantic lips and long eyelashes covering beautiful eyes below perfectly shaped eyebrows. His hands, with long slender fingers, moved gracefully when he spoke and were my favorite of all his physical characteristics. Despite the enjoyable physical aspects, it was the energy moving around Qua that drew me to him; opening something new in my heart. I knew from deep inside that divine forces were actively involved in our relationship and that the future would unfold as we surrendered into it.

Until this moment, I had not realized that for this lifetime, possibly for many lifetimes, I had yearned for something that I could not describe or identify; something beyond my grasp. From my observations, male/female relationships always seemed to end up in downward spirals. People either stay together out of need and obligation, or they end in anger and separation. It is rare to find a couple who support each other's spiritual growth while maintaining mental and physical intimacy. A strong knowing centered in my heart, telling me that Qua and I had the potential to be intimate spiritual partners for as long as we shared this earthly time together.

Qua opened his eyes and smiled. I looked away, embarrassed to have been caught studying him. Reaching over he pulled me into the warm circle of his arms.

His tone was soft and caring as he asked, "How did you sleep, Vishara?"

"Thanks for using my name. There is such power in the harmonic of a name. It evokes a wonderful frequency in me." Smiling I added, "I slept great, how about you?"

"My dreams were wild. I became totally awake in the middle of the night and saw a strange entity peeking through a misty veil of some kind. I'm pretty sure I was not supposed to see him, because he looked startled and immediately disappeared. I don't know why he was here or even what he was, but it was kind of fun catching him unaware." Qua said with the chuckle.

His experience brought a smile to my face. "I'm pretty mystified with all that is happening to us. I'm still in such an altered state of consciousness. While I know that spiritually no one is really new to anyone else, that we know each other on other levels of awareness; I have never felt a connection with another human being like the one we share. And it's happened in such a short period of time. It is fascinating."

I thought for a moment and continued, "The only experience remotely close to this one happened years ago, before Charles and I married. I met a man in a business situation. On my way to our first meeting, I was doing a visualization, imagining that our business relationship would have a positive outcome. However, instead of a business relationship, I unexpectedly became aware of the possibility that he was significant to me from previous lifetimes and that I had loved him deeply. As I approached the meeting place, I was unaware of the man personally; not his age, whether he was married, what he looked like or his personality. When I got to his office, he had not yet arrived. As I waited, I experienced energy revving up in my system. He walked into the front door with his grown son and my world literally stopped."

"Several hours later, after completing our business meeting and going to lunch, he walked me to my car. Time suddenly, and without warning, started again. Five hours had passed; I had been completely unaware of time. For the first time in my life I was experiencing unconditional love for a man. Inside, I knew that my answer to whatever question Jim asked of me was a big "Yes". Yes, I will be your friend. Yes, I will be your girlfriend. Yes, I will never see you again if that is what serves us. Yes, Yes, Yes! It was a thrill to have an experience where no part of the personal me was resisting or wanting anything in return. I was completely surrendered into my love and, therefore, was in complete service to this amazing Being. Prior to this experience, my only knowledge of unconditional love was with my daughters."

"So here I am again, experiencing this spectacular "Yes" directed at you, Qua. And, for the first time in my life it is reciprocated. I think you can see it, receive it and return it. What a glorious gift!"

Qua had listened intently. Once again, I felt the experience of my past brought into the present moment. It was as if everything in my earthly life, and Qua's, had been in preparation for this time of our joining together.

Relaxing into Qua's arms, I continued my inner reflections, remembering that many years after my business meeting with Jim; long after we'd become good friends, I asked him what he felt, when he first saw me sitting in his office.

"The first thing I noticed were your long, beautiful legs and then the rest of your body followed." He continued with a smile, "At lunch, I also became aware of you as a person and could see there was a possibility of a deeper connection. But then I walked you to your car and realized you were driving an old clunker. That, combined with the fact that you were a single mother, sent my antenna up. I was not interested in rescuing a damsel in distress, even a beautiful and intelligent one. From many past experiences, I knew the pitfalls of a man in that position."

Jim was never able to totally understand the gift of unconditional love I held for him. In the back of his mind, he always feared that I was looking for a provider and was primarily attracted to his wealth. He lived in an inner landscape of filters where he, like many other powerful men, viewed me and all women, as a game of chase, conquer and own. When I offered no resistance, he didn't know where to position this "damsel" in his life. He knew only that something he could not identify kept him engaged in seeing me for a number of years, yet, never quite knowing why. I, on the other hand, had no illusions about him; I knew his strengths and weaknesses and still continued to feel the love and acceptance beyond all reason. Even though I thought it would be incredible if he received my gift, it was not really necessary. Simply being able to feel total, unconditional love and the allowing of another person was complete in itself.

The experience of having my first child, Shannon, came vividly back into my memory. No words could describe the feeling of seeing that perfect little person just after she was born. I knew that no matter what happened in her life, no matter how our personalities blended, my love for her would never dim. For the first time, I experienced unconditional, Divine Love.

I looked up at Qua; a deep sense of lightness and peace filled me as I shifted from revere to sharing. "We have not had time to develop a human story together, and, yet, our love and connection is real, without room for doubt. I can effortlessly see you through the eyes of divinity as a Soul; as a result, the body and personality fade into the background. I'm clear that the only true, lasting love is beyond the personal, beyond the human level of ego, needs and desires."

For one illuminating moment, we looked at each other in total understanding and gratitude for the journey we shared in this earthly realm.

Later that morning we checked out of the motel and walked across the street to a small restaurant with outside seating. As it turned out, we had found "the place" for fantastic food and atmosphere that catered mostly to the local Big Sur residents.

We were seated overlooking a meandering creek that fed into the ocean nearby. The sun drenched our faces with warmth. The smells of salt water, fir trees, coffee and wonderful food, still extraordinary to this new soul, spilled through the restaurant creating an enchanted space.

Looking over the menu, I felt my mouth watering. There were so many delicious choices. Finally we narrowed it down and sat in quiet relaxation as we awaited our order and watched the play of people and nature all around us.

The meal was beyond fantastic. There was the feel of it and the way different ingredients played off each other. My biscuit with its moist layers of buttery softness, the firm snap of the apple slices as we bit into them, the tart and sweet fresh-squeezed red orange juice and the black, rich coffee with a spoon-full of honey! The taste, smell and feel of the fare were out of this world. I wondered why I had never before noticed, or taken the time to truly appreciate, the joy of slowly eating a scrumptious meal.

All too soon, Qua reluctantly broke the spell, "Well, I guess we had better get back on the road if we are going to make it to the Bay Area before dark. Are you going to fly back to Washington State from San Jose?" Qua asked with some reluctance.

Pulling from the body memories of Danielle I responded, "Yes. I guess I'd better do that. I am scheduled to be the guest speaker at a large church in Chehalis on Sunday. Plus, I just remembered that I have a meeting with the church council for dinner tomorrow evening." It felt strange to be talking about events and people I could barely remember, and it was even more difficult to realize I was going to be separated from Qua soon.

We walked companionably, back across the highway still holding hands to maintain the connection, climbed into the rented car and began our drive north once more.

Again, we found ourselves telling story after story about our two separate lives, each fascinated with the other's journey. Neither of us knew why we were sharing in such detail, but somehow it seemed necessary. At one point on the drive, we pulled into, and then backed out of, the driveway of a home that Qua once owned. In so doing, we experienced the integration of his life in that house with our life together. It was as if Qua's entire set of experiences from that time and place was a high-speed movie we were watching together. When the film ended, all that had taken place belonged to me as well as to Qua.

If Qua and I were to attempt to explain this to anyone, it was probable that some would find our inner reality delusional. Yet we knew, without doubt, it was real. Our lives were merging more deeply every moment. We were living in a parallel reality; all of Qua's soul experiences, and all of my soul and earthly experiences were happening simultaneously. Qua and I were experiencing life as if we were one being watching a movie. This was possible because we consciously identified ourselves to be Light Beings from another reality where this was a natural phenomena.

As we drove toward San Jose, I remembered attending a lecture with Deepak Chopra. He said that scientists now agree that we create our physical reality from what they often refer to as "the field". Sir John Eckles, who won the Nobel Prize in physiology and medicine, stated, "Out there is a chaos of energy soup and energy fields. Literally. We take that and somewhere inside ourselves, we create a world."

Deepak went on to give us numerous examples of how our initial interpretation of experiences actually structures the very anatomy and physiology of the body's nervous system. If you don't have a concept, or a notion, or an idea that something exists, then your nervous system won't even take it in. In other words, you will not be able to perceive it!

If people just stopped and allowed this fact to penetrate their reality, how could they continue to reject new possibilities? Every time we allow ourselves to expand into new experiences, our entire world shifts.

Arriving in San Jose that evening, we headed straight for the airport to purchase a ticket for my trip back to Washington State the following morning. My flight would get me into Seattle in mid-afternoon, leaving just enough time to pick up my car for the drive home, and then to the church council meeting with their agenda of resolving our space issue.

A deep wave of anxiety ran through me, as we left for the airport to catch my flight the next morning. I was still in an altered state and not sure how well I would function without Qua as a stabilizing presence. For the past few days, we had been in constant physical contact; always touching and, when that contact was broken, even for a moment, feeling supremely odd. Without physical contact, it was as if one part of our body was missing leaving us with a deep sense of loss.

We walked in silence toward my boarding gate experiencing extreme discomfort.

"Are you going to be all right, Vishara?" Qua asked with concern.

"Yes, I think so. We have not talked about our future. When will I see you again?"

"I think that I will turn in my rental car and fly up in the next few days. Is that OK.?"

It was odd to suddenly feel uncertain with each other. For days we had been living in present time, dealing with what was in front of us and not thinking beyond the moment. Now we were being required to take another, deeper step into the human experience.

"I'm relieved that you will be coming up soon. I honestly don't know what it is going to be like when I return to a life that I can barely remember."

We embraced for a long intense hug. My heartbeat quickened and my throat began to ache from withheld tears. Looking into Qua's eyes, I whispered, "I'll miss you."

We hugged again and I turned to hurry onto the plane; not looking back for fear of collapsing into a puddle on the already morning damp tarmac.

Chapter Sixteen

New Reality

"Everything is organically connected to everything else in
such a way that nothing is irretrievable and only a thing.
Everything is part of a single organism.
And each part "remembers" how once it, too,
was part of a great unity that had no parts."
~The River of Light, by Lawrence Kushner~

Sitting in the window seat of the plane heading back to Washington State; I was transfixed watching as we flew over the land far below. There were miles and miles of uninhabited spaces and now and then a town would appear.

I wondered why people were living in places so far from civilization. What of the people in those houses I could see that stood all alone with miles of wilderness surrounding them.

I groped for a description of the unfamiliar emotion I was experiencing. Finally I realized that, for the first time in my memory, I was feeling a deep sense of aloneness, as if I were torn in two, as if half of me was missing.

"I'm never lonely," I thought to myself. "Quite the opposite; I often yearn for isolation and quiet; free from the constraints of others. Loneliness is a foreign emotion that I had never fully understood—until now. How was I going to be

able to function in this new reality? The only person in the world that makes any sense to me is Qua. The only reality that seems familiar and real is from some other-worldly place that I miss desperately. I don't even know why this is happening. Is it temporary? Could it be permanent? Even as I asked those questions, I knew, without a doubt, that I had been traversing through space and time, life time after life time, in order to get back to my agreement; to be joined with Qua in our Divine Mission."

_____

I glanced over and noted a middle aged woman sitting across from me in the aisle seat. She was about to say something, but I quickly looked away. I instinctively knew that any interactions would require engaging in polite, meaningless social conversation and felt no compulsion to attempt a superficial conversation. A soul to soul connection was all that interested me and it did not require words. Closing my eyes, I sent the woman warmth and blessings while enjoying the flow of energy between us even though I sensed that her conscious mind was unaware of the exchange.

I kept my eyes closed until the captain's voice spoke over the loud speakers announcing that we were on approach to SeaTac Airport and were expecting some potentially rough weather. We all fastened our seat belts, put our seats in an upright position and prepared for a bumpy ride. As we approached touch-down, the wind caught the plane lifting it momentarily making it skitter sideways several strides like an energetic horse.

I became aware of a swirling current of emotions from the people around me. For a moment there was a surge of fear followed by a sense of relief, and even joy, upon hearing the thud of the wheels as they firmly gripped the tarmac and the reverse thrusters engaged to slow the plane down. A number of the passengers audibly sighed; others clapped.

"Were people preparing for a crash and felt relief when it didn't happen? Were they using their past to gage the present situation instead of sensing whether there was danger or not?" I wondered with curiosity.

"I had not sensed any real danger throughout the experience. Why had people been in a panic over a rough landing? It's sort of like going to a scary movie and filling yourself with fear over something that never happened, except on the screen. What is the attraction? Maybe it is just the rush of raw adrenalin that creates an illusion of being more alive. Or it could be a learned response of fear to anything out of the ordinary."

A flight attendant instructed us to remain in our seats until the plane came to a full stop. The whole process of disembarking, finding my luggage and taking a shuttle to long-term parking seemed like an overwhelming task with all the confusing thought forms and anxious energies I was still experiencing. Walking to my car I felt as if I was floating about an inch off the ground; the air around me soft, fluid and disconnected from this world. I wondered if I was in any condition to drive, but with no other apparent option, I loaded myself into my car and headed out.

Finally, I managed to find the on-ramp for I-5 South toward Chehalis and a vague memory of home. Taking a long, slow breath I allowed my emotions to begin relaxing and searched for a way to integrate my internal shifts. I had an hour's drive ahead of me and another hour after arriving home before leaving to meet the church council for dinner and a discussion about future plans. I wanted to use that time to regain my ability to focus on the church and find a common thread in order to relate to the council members.

Pulling into the driveway, I felt an overwhelming desire to speak to Qua. My unfamiliar internal feelings of isolation and loneliness had continued since my departure from the San Jose airport. They were in definite conflict with a sense of inner peace and joy. In my urgency to hear Qua's voice, I did not even take time to grab my suitcase out of the car. I snatched the phone in the kitchen, dialed his number and, and, when he answered immediately, felt a flood of relief.

"Hello." His voice vibrated through my whole body bringing with it a deep connectedness through the string of consciousness that bound us together.

"Qua, this is Vishara. It's wonderfully comforting to hear your voice. I just got home and could not wait another minute to call. It is so strange to be here and even more strange to be without you."

"I know. I'm feeling the same way. I've already checked out of the hotel and made reservations to fly up tonight. I'll turn in my rental car at the airport. Can you pick me up at SeaTac? I'm scheduled to arrive at 11:30 p.m."

I realized I had been holding my breath and let it out in relief after hearing that he was flying up tonight.

Thankfully, Qua sensed the energy behind my wish to have the two of us together again as soon as possible. We accepted that this urgent desire was not from a human form of "need" rather it was, and is, from knowing that the structure of being apart is counter-productive to our joint mission.

"Yes, of course. I am very happy that you are coming. I find myself filled with so many clashing emotions: ecstasy that we have found each other, a residue of concern that this is all some temporary condition and at the same time, concern that it will dissolve into the old reality. I know that it is all Spirit led and I trust in the Universe to figure it out. I have never experienced having another person be so important to my soul's journey."

"Having said all that, I am, at the same time, feeling very peaceful right under the surface of all these thoughts and emotions. Most of who I am is observing the human part with humor and fascination. In the car on the way from the airport I drove past places that are familiar to me, yet they seemed completely new. Even my relationship with this house is very impersonal.

Just last week I was busy decorating and putting my personal stamp on this environment. It is as if I am in someone else's house. It will be interesting to see how it feels to meet with the group tonight."

"Well, hang in there. I'll be with you soon and, together, we can discover what is next for us."

A smile flickered across my face. "I'm reminded of a quote from Helen Keller, *"Life is either a daring adventure or nothing at all."* By that definition, we are good examples of living life fully. I'm still surprised and pleased to be with another person who so intimately shares my journey. Until now, through the twisting paths of my life, my inner world has been a solo act. Friends have traveled along with me from time to time, but none have ever been fully engaged in the same sacred voyage. I'm anxious to be back together physically. Until then, have a restful flight. I'll meet you at the gate if I get there in time. Otherwise I'll pick you up at baggage claim."

"I love you. See you soon."

"Love you too," I said and reluctantly hung up the phone. Suddenly I realized that we had never actually spoken those words, "I love you". It felt so natural that I almost didn't notice that it was the first time.

Rushing, I fed the barn cats and hauled my suitcase upstairs dropping it just inside the door to unpack later. Then I jumped in my car to head to the council meeting. The Steak House Restaurant was a favorite meeting place with its large tables and convenient location right off the freeway. Being a vegetarian, the name never sounded very appetizing; however they had a great salad bar and good breads.

As I drove into the parking lot, I could see from the parked cars that most, if not all, members of my group had already arrived. The evening air was still heavy with moisture as I walked toward the entrance.

Five faces turned to look my way and called out greetings as I approached the table. For a moment I paused, fighting for some sense of the previous affinity that I knew I had shared with these friends. Of course I remembered them, yet my feelings toward each one was completely different than it had been just last week. It was like looking into a scene from another persons' vantage point.

"What is even more strange", I reflected, "is that I'm not experiencing much emotion; positive or negative. I feel a sense of detached observation and I'm unsure of how to behave. It's as if I'm from somewhere else."

I greeted them and slid into the large booth. The invisible new energy emanating from me had everyone at a loss for words as we looked at one another. Finally Allen broke the silence with his easy going demeanor.

"Good to see you. It was odd last Sunday without the church, but I think our congregation will be coming to your guest appearance tomorrow morning. Have you thought anymore about our next steps?"

I hesitated, knowing that words could not accurately express my new reality. "Honestly, I have no idea what will happen with the church. Over the past couple of weeks I have experienced a profound shift in my inner landscape. If I knew how to talk about it, I'd share more about it. Right now I'm in the middle of this new reality and I need time to let it settle in before making plans for the future."

"Is this about your new relationship with Qua?"

After hesitating, I replied. "No, not in the way you seem to be implying. My own Spirit is shifting my reality at a rapid rate of speed. Qua is a part of the shift; however, he was not the reason. This is based on a spiritual awakening, not a personal relationship. I know there have been rumors about a romance between us and accusations that our spending time together caused the end of Qua's relationship with Terri and my marriage to Charles. If you look at the situation through that filter, you could falsely come to that conclusion. I'm not attempting to argue for my truth, merely letting you know that this whole story is far bigger than a small town drama."

"So, why don't you just tell us the story?" Emily asked.

Looking into her eyes, I knew that anything I said at this point would only add fuel to the gossip. She, on some level, had a vested interest in perpetuating this latest drama. The talk around town had gained enough momentum to have a life of its' own. I was now playing a part in a story that had nothing to do with me or my truth.

"Emily, the only thing I can say is that what is being said is not true. If you do not trust that, then anything I add will be too easily misunderstood."

Maria, the peacemaker among us, quickly said, "I believe you. Besides, this is really none of our business. Let's just let it go and move on."

There was a chorus of agreement and sighs of relief around the table. Emily smiled in a knowing way and moved her attention back to the group.

For nearly two hours I sat and watched as these wonderful people shared stories and ideas about the future of the church, laughed together and ate from each others' plates like a big family. To the best of my ability I participated, however, it was obvious to everyone there that something was very different.

Later, I heard that they had concluded that I was just overly tired and probably still reacting to the dissolution of my marriage to Charles. Standing to leave, I looked around the table and said my goodbyes sending blessings to each person, knowing that this would probably be the last time I would meet with them in this way.

As I walked back to my car to make the drive to SeaTac airport, I became fully aware of the fact that I was now living in a world poles apart from those around me—with new rules and even different physical laws. I no longer believed that the outer world was solid and real. I could perceive the fluidity of matter and the transient nature of forms. It felt as if I were walking through a field of possibilities which only manifested into something solid when observed. I could see crystalline light particles floating like a translucent fog around everything. People appeared to be engulfed in an egg shaped cocoon the size and color of which would change with what was vivid in their consciousness.

Prior to walking into the restaurant and interacting with people other than Qua, I had not realized how much my inner landscape had shifted. With my previous ego-self no longer in control of my life; my mind was dissolving into the will of my Soul. I had stopped directing my life and was now being guided by my Higher Self. I was no longer wasting massive amounts of energy trying to make life work out in a particular way. Rather, I found myself more willing to surrender into the mystery as it revealed itself in each moment.

Light of heart, I accepted the present reality to be as it was; looking through the eyes of Divinity at the extraordinary beauty of right 'now' in the illusion of time.

Chapter Seventeen

Reunited

"All that is necessary to unify the worlds is to be aware that
it is only by an illusion that they seem to be separate at all."
~The River of Light, **by Rabbi Lawrence Kushner~**

I pulled up to the baggage claim area just as Qua walked out of the terminal. He spotted me immediately. Opening the door, he threw his bag on the back seat and climbed in beside me.

As we looked at one another, I could feel psychic energy flaring between us; all of my senses ignited the normal and the paranormal.

"I'm so glad you are here!" I said with deep feeling.

"This is definitely a first for me. How are you holding up? You seemed a little on edge when we spoke earlier today."

"I'm actually feeling quite peaceful under some pretty chaotic surface energy. Now that you are here, my emotions seem more congruent with my True Self. One thing is certain, only Divine destiny could script this journey we are on."

"I have to agree with that! How did the meeting go?"

"It was very strange for all of us. I found it impossible to relate to the people or even the church decisions, as I would have a couple of weeks ago. Basically, I let them know that my plans are on hold for now. While they reluctantly accepted my position, it was obvious to everyone that I have changed in ways that are not yet clear to them or even to me. They all seemed to be confused and, in some cases, concerned, maybe even a little angry; which is understandable given I'm a totally different soul, while they have stayed pretty much the same."

Chuckling, I added, "Tomorrow's church service will be interesting."

By the time we pulled into the driveway of my house, we were once again nearing exhaustion.

Willing our legs to move, we found our way into the house. Qua, bags in hand, followed me upstairs to my bedroom. My suitcase still sat on the floor where I had left it earlier. For a moment I wasn't sure what to do or how to act. Basically, Qua was moving in and there were no future plans for him to leave. Until this moment, he had never even been in the upstairs of my home, let alone in my bedroom. Spiritually, I knew this was exactly what we were to do, but my human self was feeling awkward, at best.

Turning to him I said, "The only way I know that our being together is right is that it just 'is'—beyond all reason or logic. The little voice in my brain is saying that before moving into the same bedroom, we are supposed to get to know each other and fall into romantic love. You are supposed to court me and we're supposed to figure out what we have in common."

Qua smiled, "Looking at it that way, it doesn't make much sense. Here you are living on a ranch in rainy Washington while I'm travelling around like a gypsy on a spiritual quest. You are a minister, of all things, and I have no interest in the whole church model. You have a ranch and house full of "stuff" while I can fit everything I own in a small U-Haul trailer. Fortunately, we are not following our mind or our logic."

"You're right. This cannot be processed through the mental body. I honestly don't see how we could begin to share these experiences with anyone else and have it understood. Juelle and Donovan are the only people who may be able to accept the truth about our being together. Most people in the community try to make sense of our relationship through a 'small story' version of 'boy meets girl, boy and girl like each other, boy breaks the heart of other girl . . . ."

"Stop, Vishara." Qua prompted with a chuckle. "We are following our Spirit and that is clearly leading us to be together. The small thoughts of others are just that, small thoughts."

I felt something inside ease. "Again, you're right. It really has nothing to do with us, unless we give it life by either resisting or fighting against the misperceptions. People are on their own journey and will think whatever makes sense to them through the filters of their own personally created reality."

My grin widened, "I suggest that we better get ready for bed and get some sleep since we have to wake up in just a few hours."

For a moment, Qua appeared confused, "We have to get up early? Oh, yes, I remember now, you're speaking at that other church in the morning."

"That's right. Aren't you glad your Spirit assigned you to a relationship with a minister? God has a sense of humor after all."

I awoke to the soft light of early dawn and the sensation of Qua's warm body next to me. Outside everything was disarmingly peaceful. The stormy weather seemed to have eased for now. Listening to Qua's gentle breathing near my ear created a sense of intimacy that was completely new in my experience. I watched him sleep, wishing we did not have to leave this enchanted space. It was not his physicality that held the attraction, even though he was fantastic to look at; it was the unique energetic signature that emanated from him that was so captivating to me.

Dragging myself, grudgingly, out of my luxurious sense of well being, I touched him gently on the shoulder.

With sleepy eyes slowly opening he responded in a soft voice, "Good morning. You're awake early."

"Did you forget again?" I said with a smile. "We're off to church this morning, unless you would like to stay in bed and catch up on some sleep?"

"No. Just give me a minute to wake up. I definitely don't want us to spend any more time apart, physically. Watching you board the airplane in San Jose and the inner turmoil I felt until we were together again is too vivid in my memory."

"I'm glad you're going to be there with me. I agree that we are much better off together. Our shared energy is an astounding force. I'll just go take a shower while you rest for a few more minutes." I said as I climbed out of bed.

"Do you want company?" Qua asked with a lazy grin.

Color bloomed in my cheeks as I swatted him lightly with my pillow and replied, "I don't think so. But I won't be long."

Snuggling back into the covers, he teased, "If you change your mind, just let me know."

I showered and dressed in a warm, deep blue cashmere sweater and dark brown gabardine slacks. Looking in the mirror, I applied a minimal amount of makeup and combed my shoulder length blond hair back from my face.

Calling out to Qua that the bathroom was all his, I went down to the kitchen, and began fixing toast and fruit, my usual breakfast, while wondering if that would be sufficient for Qua. A few minutes later, Qua walked in dressed in his usual attire. This time it was a shimmering silver pull-over top with wide sleeves narrowing at the wrists. His pants were lavender with the same fullness around the thigh narrowing at the bottom. Inside I laughed at the picture we made—me with my more traditional garb and Qua in another version of his Royal Light Command outfits.

"What are you smiling about?" he asked.

"Oh, I was just laughing at the unlikely pair we appear to be on the outside."

"Looks can be deceiving." A grin flashed across his face as he walked over and enclosed me in his arms.

Qua and I drove to the large church located in the middle of Chehalis where I was scheduled to speak. The building was old, but in good repair, with large stained glass windows down both sides of the sanctuary, high ceilings and traditional church pews. The morning light slanted through the windows and the air smelled of fresh flowers and candle wax. I loved the divine energy of the space. I looked forward to surrendering myself to the higher frequencies that I could feel building inside wanting to speak through me in service of the awakening of all.

I could not even remember why I had been invited to speak. Was their minister on vacation? Or maybe they were in between ministers. I wasn't sure of the reason but knew there was no other place I'd rather be in this moment.

Many people had already arrived. We were greeted by the church coordinator, Jillian, who gave each of us a program and asked that I be seated in a chair positioned to the right of the podium.

My eyes met Qua's, "I'll meet you after the service."

He smiled and took a seat in the back of the room. As I walked forward I could feel our energy vibrating in the space between us. Even when we were physically apart, the flow of our joined essence continued on subtle levels. I marveled, "How thin the veil between this and other worlds."

Even those who knew me did not speak. The space was too sacred to be reduced to mere words. There was an invisible energy being generated that everyone in the room could feel. The veil lifted and time seemed to shift into another dimension.

I took my seat and, as the program commenced, I looked out at the group of beautiful souls. Once again I found myself in the world where crystalline light permeating everything. There were rainbows of pastel colors and intricate designs blending with the dancing light coming through the stained glass windows. The world was a fairy tale village from a child's dreamland. Yet it was real enough to be experienced on some level by all present. As I absorbed the miracle of lights, my sense of smell and hearing was heightened. I could distinguish the scent of each variety of flower . . . roses, mixed with tulips and greens, the wax that was used to lovingly polish the aging wood, perfumes and lotions worn by the congregation, the tall bees—wax tapers on the altar, and even the air itself. Every note of the music penetrated my soul as never before.

From far away, I heard my name and realized it was time to speak. As I stood in front of the room, the silence was so intense that it seemed to pound like the drumbeat of my heart. And then, for one eternal moment, everything went completely still.

A sense of complete peace and tranquility enveloped me. I experienced a stream of consciousness in the form of a rotating, golden energy field flowing down from above, entering my body through my crown chakra and continuing down through my feet and deeply permeating the Earth. Abandoning myself to the movement, I began to free fall into an overwhelming experience of unconditional Love and Divine Service. In this energy field it truly did not matter what was being voiced verbally. The blessing was in the radiant energy itself as it reached out to lovingly envelope the room.

Language in the form of words came through me and people seemed to understand what was being said, however, the energy behind the language was all that was vivid in my experience. The frequency of Divinity was traveling out with each word and being returned in a continuous loop of spiritual energy.

Somehow I knew when my allotted time elapsed and I stopped speaking after a closing prayer and a blessing for the congregation.

The room remained absolutely silent for several seconds after I sat down. Pulling herself out of the surreal energy in the atmosphere around us, Jillian rose from her seat and began to clap. Instantly the room was standing, alive with love and applause. Laughter and tears flowed freely as people, on some level, realized that they had just experienced their own 'True Identity'.

The thin veil that separates Heaven and Earth had been penetrated for a moment in the illusion of time.

After the closing prayer and music was complete, I stood quietly and walked along the side of the room until I could once again join Qua. A few people approached wanting to speak to us then realizing quickly that words could not express their experience. Words, or any attempts to intellectually understand what had just happened, would only diminish the profound experience we all shared.

After a short time, Qua took my hand, and without a word we walked out of the sanctuary together.

Euphoric feelings filled us with the effervescent energy of being in a human body on this beautiful planet. Where we were to go from here was completely in the mystery. I could never have predicted or even imagined the events of the past month. The walk-in experience wiped out any delusions that I knew, or could in any way control, the path to my future.

Chapter Eighteen

Paradigm Shift

"Your old life was a frantic running from silence.
The speechless full moon comes out now.
A great silence overcomes me, and I wonder why
I ever thought to use language."
~by Rumi~

We were hungry. The energy from fruit and toast eaten so long ago had dissipated, but we didn't want to go to a local restaurant where we were sure to run into someone from the community who knew us or had attended the service. It would be irreverent, we felt, to try to talk about the experience we had all just shared, however, I knew that people usually attempt just that! Words can never accurately describe spiritual truths.

"Let's stop and pick up groceries and supplies on our way home so we won't have to leave the house for a couple of days if we don't want to. I'd like to spend some time integrating these radical changes and see what is next on our Spirit's schedule," I suggested.

We drove into the crowded supermarket parking lot, parked the car and entered the store hand-in-hand. I noticed that even our natural stride matched perfectly. We even started on the right foot rather than the left foot.

Sauntering down the aisles of the grocery store, everything looked so delicious that my mouth started watering with the very thought of food. I began grabbing whatever struck my fancy.

Looking at our cart, I began to giggle. "Usually eating is pretty low on my list of priorities."

"Doesn't look that way to me," Qua said with a grin and a tilt of his head toward the basket full of food.

With a bit of embarrassment, I agreed, "We are getting a lot of food for two people. Let's just grab a few things out of the Deli section and call it good." Suddenly curious, I asked, "Are you one of those men who knows his way around a kitchen?"

"No. My idea of fixing a meal is a baked potato and salad. From the amount of food you are buying, you must enjoy cooking."

"Not really, at least not every day. But when in the mood, I'm pretty good at it. I'm big on easy, fast and healthy. A baked potato and salad sounds great. Actually pretty much anything sounds wonderful right now!" I paused and then added, "I think the reason I'm piling this cart so full of foods I rarely eat is because I get ravenously hungry after spending time in high frequency energies like the one we shared earlier at the church. The same thing happens when I channel. Maybe it's my body's way of getting grounded."

"That could be. Do you think that's why I love dark chocolate?" Qua asked with a sparkle in his eyes.

Whether we were walking down the aisle of the grocery store or sitting eating breakfast at the kitchen table earlier this morning, it all felt oddly intimate. But then, everything I did with Qua seemed that way. Being together was as natural as breathing. Our journey over the past few weeks had been so intense that it felt great to be playful with each other.

Qua smiled winningly, "Shall we pack it up and head home? I'm starting to feel a little woozy from lack of food."

———————

After bringing the several sacks of groceries in from the car, we started snacking while unloading the food and putting it into the cabinets and refrigerator. By the time we were finished our hunger had been satisfied with no need to fix a meal.

With a plate of cheese, crackers, olives and fresh broccoli, we headed in to light a fire in the fireplace; Qua with his natural coke and I with my cranberry juice. A sense of peace permeated the air around us as we sat beside each other melting into the cushions and throw pillows on the couch.

With a deep sigh I asked, "So, any ideas about what is next?"

Qua considered for a moment. "It's never felt like this geographical area is right for me. I know you have built a life around this community and I feel sensitive about asking you to considering a change. Have you ever thought about being more mobile? For example, what if we buy another motor home and travel around offering workshops and channeling sessions?"

"Humm. No, I guess that never occurred to me—not that it isn't a possibility if Spirit sends us in that direction. It would take a huge amount of letting go for me to do that. I have my horses and all that goes with them plus a large house filled with furniture and 'stuff'."

Qua looked surprised, "I didn't know you have horses!"

"Oh, yes. They are a great passion of mine."

"How many do you have?" He asked with some concern in his eyes.

"I have my seven year old gelding, Kalypso, who has been with me three years and is my best buddy. And I have a new foal. Kalypso is with my trainer and the foal is boarded at a nearby farm."

"Do you see them often?"

"I take a riding lesson with Kalypso once a week and try to get over to see him much more often than that. I have not connected much with the foal. He was born in the middle of my separation from Charles, so he has not been a priority beyond keeping him safe and well cared for. I planned to fix up the small barn on this property as soon as I was settled and keep both of them here. In fact, that is why I rented this home with a barn and some land."

"Well," Qua said "I guess we'll have to figure this out as we discover what is coming next. This would be overwhelming if left up to my human mind. My life has been about simplifying and letting go of attachments, the idea of taking on more 'stuff', especially something like two horses, is not at all the direction I thought my life was taking."

For a moment fear curled deep inside me. My mind no longer had much of a hold on me but I could feel it scrambling to take back its control. *"Are you setting yourself up for a fall? Are you giving up the life you have built just to have this guy take off because you have lots of stuff or because you don't meet his expectations? Have you been floating on the newness of this reality and therefore making it possible for it to crash down around you?"*

With a huge lump starting to form in my stomach and moving quickly toward my heart and throat, I got up. "I'm going outside while there is a lull in the weather. I'd like to pick some flowers."

"Vishara, are you all right? May I come with you?" Qua said with a concerned frown.

"No, please don't. I'll be right back." I got up trying not to bolt out the door. I needed some time alone to relax into my knowing and release this build up of old mind chatter. It amazed me how much cellular memory of fear could be activated in my body. I would be in absolute spiritual awareness and then have a trigger, a word, feeling or thought, would send me spiraling down into pain. The good news is that I was always in observation behind the distortional energies.

Gardening was an activity that often brought me back to center. The smell of the soil, the beauty of plants and the creativity of putting together a bouquet of branches and flowers, was healing to my soul.

Nearing the back edge of the property, I reached over and began picking small branches from a large forsythia bush with beautiful yellow flowers just beginning to bud. My mind almost immediately became quiet as I enjoyed the soft blue skies and a breeze that held teasing hints of spring. Looking over I saw that Qua was watching me from the window. He was looking at me with devastating tenderness and concern.

Fears eased, I smiled and waved.

Walking back into the house a few minutes later with an arm full of forsythia, pussy willows and cedar branches, I received, without warning, a download of insights from my council. These came in an instant of understanding—without words—just a profound knowing.

After walking into the kitchen and putting my bouquet of branches into the sink with some water, I joined Qua and began an attempt to put into words what had just been given to me.

"I've just had another profound message from my council. I'm not sure I can put this into meaningful words yet, so this may sound a bit strange. Still, I have a feeling you'll understand."

With a knowing look and nod, Qua sought my message.

"The physical reality for most people in this time of their evolution is having their life run by a 'biological, sexual imperative'; that is, to survive and procreate. This may be conscious or subconscious but it is held in the very cells of the body. It manifests by choices made to fulfill personal needs rather than following the inner voice of Spirit leading us into the mystery."

Qua listened giving me his full attention and shaking his head in understanding.

"For many men the desire to have children, or to create something tangible that will go on in 'their name' after they leave the body, is a driving force throughout many lifetimes. This picture of reality is strongly supported by the outer world; men are expected to be successful, find a beautiful, intelligent wife to bear their children, accomplish deeds that will go down in history and have their sons continue onward with the same values."

"For many women there is a deep seated need to be valued by a male so that he will protect her and her offspring. In the body, it literally feels like survival. Women go to great lengths to maintain youth and beauty. They often seek to become 'everything' to their male partners, even giving up their own dreams, so that they will not be left for another more desirable mate."

"Fear of death is at the root of it all; death in all forms—the body, a job, relationships; even when that relationship is abusive and no longer supports happiness or evolution. The 'biological imperative' says to survive at all costs."

"In our society we pretend that death does not exist. When a person gets a life-threatening disease, we encourage them to 'fight it' and 'beat it'. We act as if our bodies are not going to die at some point; but, just like all forms, without exception, the body has a beginning, middle and end. When the Bible says that life is everlasting, the body is not included in that statement. The life force inside of us is what we are; it is the aspect of us that is everlasting. It is true that this same life force is animating our bodies while it still lives, but the bodily form will end even as the life force continues to exist; never-ending."

"When people see a marriage that has lasted for many years, they celebrate its success, even if the couple involved is miserable. Doesn't that seem crazy when you think about it?"

Qua smiled, "You'll get no argument from me on that. Truthfully, I've never wanted a wife and family. I've never even dated a woman with children for any length of time. My experience has been different in that respect from most men. I've always been looking for someone who would share a life deep with spiritual richness. In truth I had given up on that possibility until now. The women I have known usually want a traditional relationship; the house with a picket fence or some version of that scenario. That's never interested me."

I gazed at him with a multitude of emotions. Never had I met a man who wanted a relationship with me, yet did not desire the standard package of marriage. Qua quite simply undid me with his ability to relate to my way of seeing life and its possibilities. Never before had I come close to having a man understand my inner landscape. I was surprised at the way Qua and I seemed to fit together, and understand one another's heart, mind and dreams.

I continued to share my epiphany, "Our relationship is representing a new paradigm that has none of the need fulfillment elements driving it forward. Looking back, I see that we have been preparing for many years, perhaps many lifetimes, to let go of the biological, sexual imperative and surrender into this new frequency. It no longer makes sense in our inner landscape to continue in any way other than following our own Spirit wherever it takes us; knowing that we are here for something bigger than our personal small story of survival."

I searched his face to measure his response. After a moments' hesitation, he said, "I totally understand and accept the truth in this information. We are together for a reason beyond our ability to understand. Our life will unfold moment by moment. The direction it goes is being guided by a higher aspect; Spirit. I keep going into my knowing to be sure that we are continuing on this journey together, beyond the judgments of my mind. The answer is a strong 'Yes'."

I looked at him with quiet appreciation, "Knowing that we live in a Universe that understands our needs and the best direction to take our current lifetime, allows us to surrender into our higher calling above all other voices."

With that thought my expression softened. "Like you, I had totally lost any hope of finding myself in a partnership on this amazing spiritual journey in a human body. In reflection, I can see that my relationships all had their foundation in need fulfillment to varying degrees. Even Charles and I were joined mostly in support of my daughters, Alex and Shannon. Once Alex, the last one, left home, the need for Charles and me to be together as husband and wife no longer existed."

Feeling newly alive, Qua and I sat holding hands in quiet contemplation, surrounded by the warmth of the fire in this world and our spiritual councils in the unseen world. In complete peace and comfort we sat side by side, looking out the panoramic picture window as the rays of sun, getting lower on the horizon, cut through tall evergreen trees creating ribbons of light and shadow.

Chapter Nineteen

Road Trip

"Energy is what fills the universe
Energy is what comes and goes
Consciousness is what defines the energy
Under that consciousness we're each in touch with all of it."
~Das Energi, by Paul Williams~

Over the next couple of days Qua and I became inseparable, with no desire to spend even a few minutes without physical contact. The rest of the world seemed dim and very distant. We were living together in some other place; a parallel universe.

I became aware of all Qua's endearing traits; his long elegant fingers gesturing when he talked; his easy stride and quick reflexes, the way his chin jutted out when he was nervous or concentrating. And best of all, I adored his sense of humor. He used his sharp intelligence to make plays-on-words or see everyday situations as humorous. I seemed to be laughing constantly. For the first time in our adventure together, I was finding myself falling deeply in love with the human aspect of this amazing man.

Qua always appears calm and gentle with an almost stoic air, therefore, at first glance people may tend to underestimate his personal power. His strength comes from an invisible energy. He effortlessly creates results, and stabilizes people and situations wherever he directs his attention.

We no longer felt that it was odd to be assigned to each other. Our previous ideas about the forms of our spiritual calling were now open for whatever came next. Vivid in our reality was the fact that we were meant to be together. We surrendered to our future in whatever way it might unfold in this earthly world.

One evening, as I sank down on the couch beside Qua, I sensed that, as one soul and mind, it was about time for us to come out of our tranquil cocoon and consider our next steps.

Beginning the conversation, I said, "As I look into my knowing, it feels like we are supposed to be in some other geographical location, maybe just a short distance away, like Olympia. Yet I'm seeing possibilities as far east as Colorado or even south to New Mexico or Northern California. Right now it is not clear."

Smiling, I continued, "I'm hoping for Olympia. That would make everything a lot easier. We could just move the church and go on with what is already established."

Qua considered inwardly for a moment and responded, "I'm getting that we pack up and go on a journey making a big loop through Colorado, down to New Mexico and back through California. We'll know in our bodies if we find our next place."

"That will be fun! I agree, we will definitely feel when it is right. My personality is just hoping it is not Colorado or New Mexico; the places farthest away where I don't know anyone!"

Qua laughed, "I've heard that Boulder is a great community where we might fit in, and I love the idea of Santa Fe; a nice warm climate."

"I'm willing, if that is what is asked of us. I'm just putting in my request to Spirit that a long-distance move would be expensive and, from a human perspective, not very practical. We already have an established church which is on the brink of becoming large enough to be viable. It could be a launching pad for whatever expression our mission together manifests."

Qua pulled me toward him. "Vishara, there's no need to start strategizing when nothing is clear to us. Let's take off tomorrow morning. Do you think you could be ready by then?"

"I guess there's no reason to wait. After these past couple of days of rejuvenation and integration, I feel ready to get on with it. I'll call the neighbor to feed the barn cats. Otherwise, I have no commitments."

Jumping up I started toward the stairs, already packing in my mind, then turned and added, "I'm excited. Being in the car alone together while going wherever our Spirit directs will be fantastic!"

Early the next morning we loaded our suitcases and snacks into my Honda Prelude, starting our journey by heading north to Olympia, WA. We stopped for breakfast at a wonderful restaurant across from a park in the middle of the city.

As we sat eating a scrumptious organic meal, I really focused on allowing this to be the place for us to settle. It had all the ingredients; not too big, a beautiful town with great restaurants and shops, quite a large community of progressive thinkers and—it would be an easy, affordable move. Plus, the community from Chehalis could easily drive an hour to participate in events.

By the end of breakfast and a walk in the park, we knew that this was not for us. The frequencies of the town did not feel in harmony with our mission. There was no logical explanation; we just knew that this was not our next home-base.

Resigned, we got back in the Honda, Qua in the driver's seat, and headed south to Portland, Oregon where we could catch the highway running east along the Columbia Gorge toward Boise, Idaho. The scenic drive was breathtaking. The sky was a brilliant blue backdrop for the high cliffs rising up on either side of the wide Columbia River. Green vegetation, just beginning to wake up after a long winter's nap, was peeking out among the rock formations. Because of the recent storms and overflowing dams, the river itself was full of fast-moving water beautifully demonstrating the power of nature.

Holding Qua's hand and relaxing back into the seat, my mind began to wander, accessing Danielle's past.

———————

Qua and Danielle first met in Sedona at a weekend event led by a spiritual group called Earth Mission. Danielle was a key player in this group for a number of years prior to the time Qua became involved. Earth Mission was led by two dear friends who channeled amazing teachings with an emphasis on self discovery of our True Identity and multiple dimensional realities. This unique pair was Danielle's first experience with new souls walking into an adult body.

Like so many teachings and groups, some of the participants claimed to be walk-ins. It was quite easy to detect those who were truly walk-ins and those who just pretended because of their egoic desires. Having a soul rotation is not a common occurrence nor is it the highest spiritual possibility for most people.

Soul rotation, or walk-ins, can be quite dangerous if a person without a pure intent and the mark of destiny opens themselves to channeling or having another soul rotate into their body. There are bodiless forces and entities in the unseen world that will happily live through the ego of an individual currently inhabiting a human body. Once they take hold, the person possessed can become addicted to the power being generated through them and lose their own identity. This has happened throughout human experience. In extreme cases, church leaders have been brought in to do an exorcism, sometimes with success, sometimes not.

Becoming a pure channel, or walk-in, is pre-destined and based on agreements that were made prior to birth. In these cases, the purpose is to assist in the evolution of this earthly reality.

Danielle had never considered the possibility that she would be a channel or have a walk-in experience. With Danielle's strong, charismatic personality it seemed highly unlikely that she would step aside to allow other souls to use her body. She had continually assessed the situation and determined that these experiences required a level of surrender that she neither had nor wanted.

I found myself drifting off to sleep and woke up with a jolt as Qua maneuvered around a car.

"Oh, my gosh. That startled me. I guess I fell asleep."

"Sorry I woke you. A car in front was going dangerously slow and someone else was right on my tail."

"No problem. I want to be awake. We're almost out of the Columbia River Gorge and I missed some of my favorite scenery."

I wondered out loud, "Did you do any work to discover your 'Divine Essence' or your 'Divine Function' when you were with the group in Sedona?"

"Yes. I discover that my Divine Essence is 'Evolution'. Most people think of Evolution as a way out of the human condition. From my knowing, it is just the opposite. It is a frequency to be brought into the world of form, not a strategy to evolve out of this dimension."

"I also know that my Divine Function is "Structural Integrity". If you stop to think about it, the 'Force of Evolution' has total integrity with All-That-Is. I can feel any lack of balance in situations, people, even in physical structures. That's one of the reasons I don't let many people get close to me physically unless there is a certain level of integrity in the exchange. I find all the hugging that goes on pretty uncomfortable."

Laughter sparkled in my eyes. "I can see what you mean. There can be some pretty weird energy exchanges in the guise of a hug."

"Juelle and Danielle, in their Wednesday night gatherings, assist people in the discovery of their Function and Essence. It definitely elevates an individual's personal identity and can make a rather dramatic spiritual shift. We found that the most effective way for most people to discover their deepest truth, was to ask them what behavior they had been criticized for their whole life. Because individuals are taught from early childhood to look for what is wrong with themselves and others and try to correct it, most people have been condemned for expressing their divine essence and function."

"For example, Danielle's divine essence was 'Inspiration'. Just by being in her presence, people would be inspired. She had been criticized for being too enthusiastic and not grounded. Her ego's reaction would be to constantly attempt to inspire people to see things her way and would instead be looked upon as a 'space cadet' by those who were more serious or quiet."

"I can see that." After a short pause, Qua asked, "What is your Divine Essence?"

"I've not considered that question yet. Give me a moment and I'll see what is revealed."

Closing my eyes and relaxing into my knowing, I asked my higher Self, "What is my divine essence? Of all of the qualities of the God Mind, which one do I value above all others? It could be wisdom, truth, justice, freedom, love or any number of other words describing a quality of the "I Am" mind. While I value all of these, what is the one aspect that is my essence? Almost instantly I knew it to be "Creation". Without the experience of creation, my life would not be worth living. I would no longer have a sense of purpose or a vehicle through which to express. I felt a flood of pleasure as I embodied the essence of Divine Creation.

Opening my eyes I shared my insight with Qua. He smiled and shook his head up and down in agreement.

"So, what is your function?"

Again, I went to that quiet place inside and asked the question. The immediate response was the sentence, "I am here to exalt the essential nature of the Is-ness".

Looking at Qua I repeated what had been given to me.

He looked a little confused. "I sort of understand. But please tell me what it means to you."

"It feels very clear in my body. I am here to assist in the awakening of individuals and the awakening of this earthly world into a new reality; a new world. I am here to co-create a world that embodies a high frequency of expression; one that has never before been experienced on Earth."

As I was talking, waves of understanding and future possibilities were being downloaded.

"We are on the brink of an Awakening like never before in the story of mankind. The two of us are joining with many others who are arriving on-planet to assist the transformation."

For an instant time went still in that magical way that it did when Qua and I merged into one integrated whole entity.

Chapter Twenty

Moving Energy

"I said to my soul be still,
and wait without hope
wait without thought . . . .
So the darkness shall be the light,
and the stillness the dancing."
~T.S. Eliot~

We continued travelling through Oregon turning toward Boise, Idaho. We had heard that Boise was a great place to live. So we exited the freeway and drove through the downtown area and then into a section of historic homes. Lovely as it was, nothing in us said, *"This is the place."* So we turned around and got back on the highway.

As we drove southeast the towns became few and far between. Other than breaking for a quick meal around 3 p.m. and a couple of gas stops, we had been on the road since early morning and it was now approaching 9:00 p.m. The hours had flown by. Mostly we traveled, side by side, in silence, always touching; a single energy field engulfing us. If one could look down from above with eyes able to track energy, it would be apparent that our joined frequency was creating a sacred ribbon of light as we moved across Oregon and Idaho.

Looking up ahead, I noticed a billboard that said, "Accept Jesus As Your Savior; The Only True Path to God!"

With curiosity I asked, "I know you are not religious, but do you believe in God?"

Qua thought for a moment before answering, "Due to the limitations of language, people tend to describe the Light, or God, as separate from themselves. Ultimately, I do not think an entity named God exists outside of a belief system promoted by churches. When we have profound spiritual experiences it is because we have allowed our awareness to expand to more subtle perceptions and a more vast space; the Absolute, Pure Consciousness and, yet, we remain in our physical body. Even Galaxies or any other form that you can describe as having physical attributes, contain more density than the Oneness, or what many term as "God". All forms, including words, by definition exist in separation. However in this reality we often use words. In doing so we must provide some context or description to tell the story of the non-story. That was probably the original thought behind the word, God."

My heart quickened, *This is truly amazing to be with a partner who is so closely attuned to my deepest spiritual truths. I find it intriguing to hear him articulate these universal principles through his brilliant spiritual intellect in an almost poetic language. Like me, he is fascinated with the bigger spiritual meaning of any situation; always looking for a higher truth.*

I said with deep appreciation, "I am totally aligned with your thinking. Many people seem to hold God as a man on a throne that has the authority to stand in judgment of who is bad or good; who goes to Heaven and who is condemned to Hell. As I'm sure you agree, Heaven and Hell are not places outside of this reality; rather they are created by states of consciousness. It is Hell to exist in fear; it is Heaven to exist in Love."

"I think of God as a frequency representative of the Oneness as the all-powerful force in the Universe (One Verse). Of course, minimizing God to an all-knowing man is a very effective way for those in powerful positions to control others. Many churches, as well as groups from religious traditions around the world, promote this way of thinking and warn of dire consequences for those who do not follow a specific belief system. And, of course, there are the cults that have sprung up with a focus on some charismatic person asking people to surrender their power and possessions in the name of God. It is all based on a foundation of fear."

Looking over at me with agreement, Qua added, "What really amazes me is how much the Christian groups fight among themselves. You would think, given that they are all studying the Bible and the teachings of Jesus, they would at least support one another."

I shrugged my shoulders in resignation, "Of course it is all just a game of pretending to be separate from the One. In the end, everyone and everything will surrender and return Home. No one can escape being who they already are! Evolution is an unstoppable force."

For a time we sat together in silence as we continued to absorb through our thoughts and emotions some of the distortional energy around religious beliefs.

I continued, "One of the ways the teachings of Jesus are distorted by religious groups is, in my opinion, by interpreting the Bible in human rather than spiritual terms. For example in Matthew 10:34-38 Jesus says:

"Do not suppose that I have come to bring peace to the earth.
I did not come to bring peace, but a sword.
For I have come to turn a man against his father,
a daughter against her mother,
a daughter-in-law against her mother-in-law
a man's enemies will be the members of his own household.
Anyone who loves his father or mother more than me is not worthy
of me; anyone who loves his son or daughter more than me is not
worthy of me."

If you interpret these passages as referencing the personal human, named Jesus, this would seem pretty egotistical to ask people to forsake their own family to follow a person, Jesus. Rather, we have a relationship with Jesus as a Divine Being. As such, He is asking us to turn from being led through life by our personal relationships and surrender into a higher calling, that of our Spirit. He is asking us to love our divine nature, our spiritual family, above that of our human nature or our human family."

Qua sat quietly for a while. "I can see what you're saying. I just never thought to interpret the Bible in that way. It has always been presented as surrendering to a path—the only way through which you could achieve spiritual liberation—leaving me questioning a lot of the teachings. I always wondered about all the millions of people in other religions. Were they condemned to Hell because of their religious choices; and what about all the conflicting versions of the Bible?"

As we talked, I noticed that my body and emotions were feeling tremendous amounts of fear running through every cell. By focusing my energies on the distortions around the teachings of Jesus and God, I was tapping into a religious war zone. All living things are connected with a matrix made up of strains of consciousness. As a result, everyone is affecting everyone else through the frequencies emanating from their inner truth. Where attention goes, energy flows. That is why it isn't effective to end something by fighting it. When you resist anything, you are giving it your attention and therefore making it stronger.

Looking over at Qua, I said, "I'm starting to feel a little strange so I'm going to move some of this negative energy to the Light. Since you are driving, will you just hold me in your consciousness as I release these untruths that have accessed us?"

"I'll be glad to, Vishara. Let me know if you need assistance and I'll pull off the road."

"OK."

Closing my eyes I allowed myself to feel the sensations in my body that had begun to build when I read the Jesus sign and continued to develop as Qua and I discussed the negative aspects of religious zealots.

Since most of my body's personal experiences of church—as representing "religion" had been very positive, I was surprised at the level of pain in my heart and solar plexus. The only explanation was that I was being used to move negative energy in the matrix for many other people—not just for the two of us.

In my minds' eye I could see the planet with nations at war, people being persecuted or filled with self-loathing in the name of God and sainted beings such as Jesus. I allowed my body to gather up as much as I could bear to hold and started the process of opening myself to the Light through my crown chakra at the top of my head.

I could feel Qua's councils enfolding me with protection and love as the negative energies flowed up and out in a steady stream. It looked like interwoven webs, as fine as a spider's, in various hues of black and grey with an occasional red strand; all representing thought forms and emotions.

Although it only took about five minutes, it seemed much longer. Finally I felt most of it was gone. To be sure, I took a last look around in my body and released any residue I found lurking in dark corners.

For a moment I remained in this altered state of conscious opening my heart and soul in prayer, "I request my own Divine Spirit to fill the empty spaces left by the release of distortional energies with new pictures of reality, insights and spiritual awareness. I release to the Light any energy in the form of thoughts and beliefs that does not support this request. And So It Is! Thank you God."

Slowly I opened my eyes and looked over at Qua.

"How did it go?" he asked. "It felt like a ton of dense, dark energy moved. If there had been a safe place to pull over, I would have been able to help more."

"I'm just fine. I could feel your Council around me the whole time. Knowing I had our combined force at work, made it possible for me to embody a huge amount of negativity before moving it to the Light. Mostly I didn't even know what the thoughts and emotions were; I could just feel their power."

Feeling depleted and laying my head back on the seat, I said with a yawn, "Guess we had better find a place to spend the night pretty soon."

"I agree. Before we started this clearing process, I'd been looking for a place but all I've seen are truck stops." Qua looked over at me and said with laughter in his voice, "I'm thinking a truck stop is not what you have in mind?"

I smiled warmly, "I don't need anything fancy. But, you're right; I'd rather sleep in the car than in someplace unclean with well used mattresses and high levels of polyester in the bedding. That's not my thing."

After another half an hour of driving with no towns or signs indicating anything was between us and Salt Lake City, we saw what looked like a small oasis in the middle of nowhere. As we approached, we recognized it as a motel complex with a restaurant, nicely landscaped grounds and, most importantly, a 'vacancy' sign.

Pulling up in front of the office, Qua went in to register while I waited in the car. We stopped in the motel's restaurant and ordered a couple of salads and a tuna sandwich to take with us. Once we were in the room, I looked over at the bed and sighed with pleasure.

"It seems like we have established a pattern of pushing our bodies until we are absolutely exhausted. After I eat a few bites of salad, I'm heading straight for the shower. I'll be asleep the moment my head hits the pillow."

Qua grinned. "That process we did in the car probably took a lot out of you. I'm not quite ready to call it a night. Do you mind if I turn on the T.V.?"

"Sure, go ahead. I've been without a T.V. for years so I don't even know what programs are on the air." I said as I walked toward the bathroom.

"Really? Why didn't you have a T.V.?"

I turned with a sleepy smile, "Just didn't want one I guess. I can't remember why not. I do have a T.V., the one we used to watch the *'Starman'* video, but no cable or dish hook up. You go ahead. Nothing, not even the TV, will disturb my sleep tonight."

After my shower I finished getting ready for bed and crawled in beside Qua who was propped up against pillows watching a science show. I felt so tired that my muscles ached; however, sleeping with the T.V. on was far more challenging than I had expected. It gave off a frequency that I found quite disturbing. Remembering back, I always felt that same uncomfortable vibration when Charles had a computer in the bedroom.

Sitting up and arranging my pillows beside Qua, I joined him in watching the science show. I was relieved when I noticed that he was starting to dose off. Reaching over for the remote, I turned off the screen and the lamp beside the bed. After Qua rearranged himself under the covers, we snuggled and were instantly asleep.

———————————

Awakening refreshed the next morning and finding a beautiful sunny day awaiting us, we completed our morning ritual, packed and were down in the hotel restaurant ordering breakfast by 7:30 a.m.

As we sat waiting for our food to arrive, I noticed groups of young teenage girls arriving with their mothers who were hovering over them for some unknown reason. The energy in the room was unfamiliar to me. From the looks being exchanged, it seemed this was a competitive relationship. The mothers were fussing with the girls' hair and clothing; while instructing them on proper posture and behavior.

"Qua, what do you think is going on with that group of people?" Turning his head and noticing the group for the first time, he replied, "Looks like some kind of beauty pageant."

Gradually, accessing the cellular memories in my body, I remembered about the existence of beauty pageants. Yet nothing in me could relate to this strange behavior. The last time I had been born into a body was in a matriarchal society where this type of ritual did not exist.

Allowing old memories in, it began to all make sense. In the time of matriarchal domination women lived separately from men in large dwellings or temples. When it was time to mate in order to procreate, we invited men to a ritualistic gathering and chose among them for the one evening. The female children born from these unions would remain with the women until adulthood. The male children were sent to live in the male quarters once they were old enough to work.

The matriarchal society was extremely off-balance toward the feminine just as the patriarchal society of today is off-balance toward the male aspect. Men, in the matriarchal society, were considered less than women.

Processing information through the intellect was not valued. Intuition and the ability to contact inner knowing was the highest expression. Females were known to have a closer connection to spiritual realms. Men felt that they had to go through a female to evolve, yet were denied access.

After years of growing unrest among the males, they began to fight back with the one thing they had over the female—superior strength. For the first time in the human experience, wars broke out. Women were raped and held hostage. Their lands were taken, thousands were burned at the stake and those who continued with their rituals were considered witches and killed. Out of the rubble, a patriarchal society was born that still exists today. The leaders of this revolution created religious organizations around the world with teachings that denounced, as evil, anything that cannot be explained through the intellect, and, extended that edict to all expressions that are primarily feminine in frequency. Fear and hatred of the unknown became accepted as a valid reaction to psychics, healers, channels or anyone claiming to possess powers from the unseen world.

I realized that any 'beauty pageant' is a cry for acceptance in a world that honors female innocence and beauty while fearing its' potential power over men. The strange energy being projected was a survival mechanism in the very cells of these women's bodies. The mother's, knowing that their time of innocence and beauty had passed, subconsciously feared their future possibilities of aloneness and rejection. The girl's, sensing that there was power in their youth, yet resenting being seen only for their beauty, were caught between their resentment and their desire to be named the most beautiful in the group.

I could sense that Qua was feeling uncomfortable. While I would normally share my insights with him, something in me knew that this was to be held close until I had a chance to observe more of the workings of this male world I now inhabited. With my new awareness I suspected that it would be difficult for Qua to relate, given he was currently in a male body with cellular memories from a male perspective.

We finished our breakfast in silence, while I continued to study the fascinating interactions of these females. It almost made me laugh knowing the power that sat right under the surface, yet they scrambled to make themselves beautiful to the outer world, thinking their very survival depended on it!

Chapter Twenty One

The Energy of Places

"Whether or not you notice the otherworldly sensations
that mark the heightened stages of transformation,
there will be no doubt that a deep sense of inner awakening
has at last begun."
~Oneness, by rasha~

As we drove toward Salt Lake City the landscape began to change from flat farm land to rolling hills and eventually on toward the majestic Rocky Mountains reaching across the endless blue sky. While we were in awe of the geography, the energy of the area was at odds with our frequency. After turning east just past Salt Lake City, we drove on without stopping. After about an hour, I suddenly took a deep breath and realized that uncomfortable psychic energy had been cascading through me for quite some time creating shallow breathing as well as tension through my shoulders and upper back.

"Qua, how are you doing?"

As he looked over at me with slightly unfocused eyes, he seemed to be returning from a distant place. "I'm good. Guess I was space traveling. That whole area we've just driven through felt very odd. I'm not sure why."

I agreed with a shake of my head, "Have you ever noticed that towns, cities or even neighborhoods have uniquely different personalities that you either resonate with or find uncomfortable? Two towns can be just a few miles apart and yet the people and businesses that they attract are completely different."

"I guess I had never thought about it, but I can see that you're right."

I continued, "One of the ways people in this reality are being veiled to the memory of their natural ability to listen to the inner voice, or Spirit, is that the outer world of form is valued over the invisible world of energy and frequency. In truth, people cannot help but react to the invisible forces at play within everything, even places like cities and towns. The only question is how much an individual is consciously aware of these influences. Our experience over the last hour or so is a prime example. The scenery was spectacular, yet we were very uncomfortable energetically."

We drove on in silence through miles of differing terrain with an occasional small community. There were amazing rock-formed mountains and formations created by wind and sand over millions of years. We went through valleys where wild grasses and flowers defied the elements and grew, fighting their way out of the rocky soil and still chilly early spring temperatures. We consciously opened our awareness to the different frequencies we felt. In so doing we shared and received energies with these areas and the life forms inhabiting them, leaving in our wake positive streams of consciousness.

On the third day of travel, we stopped in the small community of Georgetown, Colorado for lunch. This quaint municipality sits in a valley between towering mountains. The history and energy of the pioneers and miners still inhabited the brick and stone buildings dating back to the 1800s; now mingling, energetically, with new housing, shops and restaurants.

"It's like walking into the past." Qua commented.

"I can actually feel the consciousness of that time in history where people worked hard to survive and knew very little about anything that existed outside of their small communities," I added.

"Personally," said Qua, "I can't even relate to those times. This is my first incarnation into a body."

I studied Qua for a moment. "I can easily see how that first time experience fits with many of your characteristics—even physically."

He chuckled, "Why do you say that?"

"I've never met anyone like you. Unlike most males in this reality, you have an interesting combination of male and female energy. Your physical body is highly sensitive, like that of a female, while your emotional body is exceptionally male. Your mental body seems to be a combination of both; a fascination with your spiritual nature, yet your chosen career is that of an analytical engineer. On the other side you are expressing creativity through photography and music. You are the first man I have experienced who isn't strongly motivated by his sexual urges and desires. You treat your sexuality more like most women. You are discerning and value the quality of a relationship over the sexual act itself."

"I suppose you're right. Maybe that is why I don't cultivate male friends very easily. The typical interactions between guys, mostly through competitiveness of some kind, do not match my inner landscape. I learned to play the game while working in the corporate world. It is like being an actor in a play. The character cares about goals, objectives, winning and climbing the corporate ladder, but to the actor playing the part, other, deeper values are more important. This was true even before my walk-in experience. But it all feels like another lifetime."

Walking toward the end of the historic main street, we noticed a restaurant in an old house on the edge of town. It looked like a historic house, and was crowded with other tourists, with a few locals mixed in. Seeing a sign saying

"Seat Yourself", we found a table on the patio just to the right of the front entrance into the building and sat enjoying the sunshine. When the young energetic server arrived to take our order, I asked for a garden burger with lemonade and Qua a cheese burger with coke.

The service was casual and friendly and soon we were enjoying a scrumptious meal. It was easy to see why this place was so popular.

Back on the highway we continued our descent through the Rocky Mountains into the Denver, Colorado area.

"Vishara, should we take a look at Boulder?" Qua asked.

"I've always heard good things about the Boulder community. It is supposed to be filled with very health conscious, outdoorsy types; there's most likely a substantial alternative community. It sounds like a place that would embrace our spiritual path."

"It definitely could be a town worth checking out. Let's keep a lookout for a highway sign." Qua said.

As we neared Denver, the freeway split—one way went toward Boulder and the other continued east. We took notice of the signs—yet a particular "something" refused to allow us to move to the left hand lane to head north toward Boulder. We just kept driving and soon found ourselves heading south on Hwy. 25 away from Denver.

"Well Qua, maybe my concerns about being asked to move to Colorado were unfounded. So far, it does not feel like the place for us."

"I'm not feeling anything at all; can't even get off the freeway to check it out." Qua replied

"Truthfully, I'm relieved. Inside I was pretty sure Colorado was the place."

"I was feeling the same thing. I didn't want to say it out loud and add energy to the possibility. This would not be my choice of places to live. I think of Colorado as a very conservative state where we may not be accepted and may even be feared by some religious groups."

"Of course we have a ways to go before getting out of Colorado and into New Mexico. There is Colorado Springs; however, I know very little about that area. Maybe we're being sent to Santa Fe or Albuquerque." I mused.

Qua smiled warmly, "That would be fine with me!"

I rolled my eyes, "You just want to get to a warmer, dryer climate. Guess we'll have to wait and see. I'm positive, like everything else on our journey together, that we will know when we get there."

For several miles I silently wondered about our destination and then allowed my mind to wander in and out of possibilities. Finally I broke the peaceful silence with a question of curiosity, "Qua, what first brought you to Sedona and the Earth Mission group?"

"That's a long story and one of the most powerful experiences of my life."

"We have all the time in the world," I said with a smile, "I'd love to hear it."

He began, "The major shifts that preceded my walk-in experience started while I was still living and working in Silicon Valley, I was becoming increasingly 'awake'. I was beginning to have glimpses through the veils, and yet I was in deep conflict as I tried to reconcile the common reality of my career and relationships with my increasingly expanded consciousness. Having read a book entitled "E.T. 101: The Cosmic Instruction Manual", a very insightful book about spiritual awakening, I decided to contact the author, Zoev Jho, and scheduled a one-on-one private session with her in Sedona. I was very excited, but didn't have any preconceived expectations."

"I'm friends with Zoev Jho. We call her by her nickname, Zeej" I said with a smile. 'E.T. 101' is fabulous! She has such a superb intellect and sense of humor."

"That's cool that you know her! Well, to continue, when I arrived at Zoev Jhoe's home, I was greeted by two very androgynous and attractive women.

They were dressed in pastel colors with bright symbols on the front of their tops—quite a contrast to my Silicon Valley chinos and button down shirt. When I asked about Zoev Jho, I was very disappointed to find out that she was not there and that these two were house sitting for her. Since I had traveled all the way from California to Arizona with a friend, I decided to take these rather extraordinary women up on their offer to have the private session with them.

They sat opposite me on a sofa in a living room with modern décor. It all began with what seemed like casual get to know each other conversation. But I noticed that only one of the women was speaking and the other seemed to be in meditation with her eyes closed. She was rocking back and forth slightly.

They asked what I valued most. One of the words that came to me without conscious thought was "integrity".

They asked, "What do you think integrity means?"

I replied, "Well, you know, being reliable, upholding your commitment, doing what you say you are going to do . . . . but as I elaborated I felt these common words starting to lose their meaning and energy.

"Oh!" the leader said "So that's what you think integrity means!" Somewhat taken aback, I glanced at the woman in meditation still rocking back and forth slightly.

Suddenly it became clear and I knew that integrity had nothing to do with the superficial behaviors I had mentioned, and that it had everything to do with being true, at all times, to Spirit, God, and your Inner Knowing, regardless of preferences or customs.

The power and truth of this flash of awareness was so profound that it was as though it had triggered a post hypnotic suggestion from another reality. I felt like someone had picked up a loose thread from my mental constructs about the world, and started pulling it—unraveling everything I thought I knew—and I had mistakenly thought I knew a lot!"

I listened to Qua with fascination, "For me, integrity would not be a place to access my deepest fears or inflexible structures in consciousness. I would be more likely to have a trigger point around creative expression. I love to discover the specific and unique ways we are each designed to serve our mission on earth."

"I can see that in you. But this was the key belief system that opened me to a major shift in consciousness. I couldn't speak; I began to tremble. My mind was 'blown', as if I had taken some kind of psychedelic drug. As this quickening went on, I couldn't respond to any questions my two earthly guides might have been asking me. My body felt like it was filling with crystalline light. My eyes felt like they had never been so wide open, yet they were streaming with tears because of the unknown transformation of my entire psyche—and maybe my body too. This was truly an astounding experience."

"After some time had passed—probably five or ten minutes, but I had no way of knowing—they helped me up off my chair and into a small bedroom where I could lie down. They put on an audio tape of vocalizations (toning) and drumming that only seemed to bring more waves of quickening, or increased spiritual frequencies."

Gradually the peak of the experience subsided. Apparently the time for what had begun as a private session had come to its end. Fortunately for me, my travel partner had come with the car to pick me up.

My voice and body were still reverberating with chills. My friend helped me get my things together, pay the session fee, and get ready to leave. I was able to hear the two women telling my traveling companion about some friends in Sedona that I should see while I was in town. Still in a much altered state, I accepted a note with names and number, and nodded a thank you. The trip back was a complete blur due to my extremely heightened senses and the feeling that my entire being was in a free fall upward into unimaginable realms."

I thoughtfully assimilated Qua's story and after a moment, "Wow! What a great experience. So, did you begin working with the Earth Mission group regularly after that?"

"Yes. That experience led me to the clothing and to the channeled sessions with the Earth Mission founders, KemDara and Drakar and, ultimately, to first meeting Danielle in that 3-day event. You remember that, don't you?"

Smiling I said, "Of course I remember. Those events were amazing. The channeled material and toning that came through KemDara and Drakar changed my inner world completely. The sounds generated through KemDara's exquisite voice would float through the room on wings of energy, pulling everyone present into higher and higher levels of awareness. As you know, music and toning has a power that bypasses thought."

"Yes" Qua agreed. "I have loved sound and music my whole life. I can listen to a choir singing old hymns in German and be brought to tears. The Earth Mission toning gives me that same deep connection to my spiritual essence."

With a nod of understanding I continued, "I'm sure that the many sessions I experienced over several years, prepared my energetic body for channeling and for the walk-in experience. I spent lots of time with them. In addition to the group events, KemDara and Drakar were guests in my home for days at a time and I would go to Sedona to stay with them. We worked together developing some of their later seminar materials and they used some of the Zantron channeled materials in their newsletters."

Qua looked at me in surprise. "I didn't know you were involved to that extent. Very cool!"

———

Coming back to present time, we noticed that we were entering the outskirts of Colorado Springs and started seeing signs for their places of note, like the Air Force Academy, New Life Church, Radiant Church and signs with "Focus on the Family" messages.

"Seems like there are lots of huge churches in the area and I had not realized that the Air Force Academy is here," I commented.

"I didn't know about the churches, but I did know the military has a big presence in this area. Just south of Colorado Springs is the Cheyenne Mountain Government facility where they constantly watch for incoming missiles. I think that is where the President is taken in case of an emergency. This is also the home of the Olympic Training Facility." Qua said.

"Wow. What a diverse group. The energies certainly will be interesting to observe. You know, I think 'Focus on the Family' is that born-again group led by James Dobson."

Qua groaned, "Hope we are passing right on through this area."

I felt a chill of unease.

As we drove further into the heart of Colorado Springs, we noticed an exit sign, "Manitou Springs, Valley of the Gods". We knew instantly that this was a place to visit, not only because of the name, which was intriguing in itself, but because of an inner knowing that pulled us toward the exit.

We found ourselves on Hwy. 24 and took the first exit into a community of older homes and small shops. Almost immediately we noticed a bookstore named "Conscious Living".

"Let's go into that store to ask a few questions." I suggested.

Finding a parking place on the street a block away, we climbed out of the car and headed toward the store.

"It feels so good to stretch my legs. Qua, maybe it's time to take a break and stay somewhere for a day or so?"

"I'm up for that, but I'm not sure that Colorado Springs is where we want to stop for any length of time. It may not suit our consciousness and our coming assignment."

Opening the door into "Conscious Living", we smiled at one other. The store could have been located in any spiritual community. We felt at home with the collections of incense, crystals, whimsical art, candles, jewelry and, of course, spiritual books and tapes. The colors and smells felt inviting to our senses; we walked around paying special attention to the stones and crystals that attracted us.

As we studied a beautiful faceted amethyst, a middle-aged woman with an angelic smile walked over to us and said, "Just let me know if you have any questions. There is a reading room and fresh herbal tea in the back if you want to sit for a while."

"Thanks." Qua said. "We were passing through this area and we're curious about it. Is there a large spiritual community here?"

She laughed, "There are lots of churches for sure! The more alternative people seem to gravitate to this particular neighborhood. It is not very big compared to the fundamentalist Christian groups. However we are growing in numbers."

"Where and what is the Valley of the Gods?" I asked

"It is located up the road a few miles. There are some beautiful red rock formations as well as Manitou Hot Springs. That area was considered sacred by the Indians. The red rock area is now a protected State Park."

"Sounds like our kind of place." I said to Qua, "Let's check it out."

Chapter Twenty Two

New Home Base

"Earth's cycle of condensing in a downward spiral
is reversing itself according to the Divine Plan.
This changes the game for all on the planet.
Beings are now able to reverse their focus into
an upward spiral of Spiritual Awakening."
~Zantron~

Driving toward the small community of Manitou Springs, we noticed an on-ramp that would take us back on Hwy. 24 going west toward Woodland Park.

"I think we are supposed to get back on the highway." Qua said.

"Feels that way to me too."

Instead of checking out Valley of the Gods, we found ourselves heading toward Woodland Park, another 15 miles up into the mountains at a nine thousand foot elevation.

A flicker of anticipation, as well as a chill of unease, moved through me. "Because I feel so resistant to moving to this area, I'm going to do a little prayer. I'll ask for tangible, definitive signs showing us that this is, or isn't, our next place."

"Good idea!"

I closed my eyes while sitting in an open posture and took a moment to relax any tension in my body and clear my mind. I requested that we be shown clear and decisive signals as to why we are so drawn to visit Woodland Park.

Upon opening my eyes the first thing I saw was a stand of tall Aspen trees with new leaves of bright golden green twinkling in the wind; illuminated by the setting sun. The sight filled my body with immense joy. I sat quietly bathing in the frequency and could not think or speak. Qua also seemed very peaceful sitting beside me as we drove up the mountain.

Could this be my sign? I'm not absolutely sure.

As we entered the small town of Woodland Park I wondered out loud, "Do you think there is room for a liberal thinking church in this town?"

Qua shrugged and said, "Let's drive around a bit. It would be cool if we found a little old church building to rent. You know, picture perfect with a steeple and stained glass windows." Grinning, he asked, "Would that be a 'yes' sign for you? "

We turned right onto the next side street and there it was; a small charming church made out of stone with a steeple, stained glass windows and large double doors painted red. It was surrounded by tall Aspen trees and, except for its run-down condition, looked exactly as Qua had described.

"Wow. There it is! I wonder if it is being used." I exclaimed.

"That is pretty much what I was imagining." Qua murmured.

We were a little nervous. There was no doubt that this was a clear sign; a "yes" to my query.

"Could this be the place?" Qua asked.

"I'm sensing it is. There is no doubt that seeing the church right after you mentioned it is remarkable. Also, when I opened my eyes after asking for clarity, the first thing in my vision was the Aspen trees. They seemed to be calling to me and waving us forward. It was more of a feeling rather than an obvious sign. The church is too tangible to ignore."

"OK. Let's take a breath. I noticed a small restaurant on the main road. We can circle back and stop for dinner," Qua said quietly.

After ordering a dinner of vegetable soup and salad, we sat in quiet contemplation.

I suddenly realized that I was holding my breath and looked over at Qua with amusement glimmering in my eyes, "This reminds me of an Amelia Earhart quote, *Courage is the price that life exacts for granting peace.*"

With a smile, Qua agreed, "Moving here is definitely a stretch. The good news is that it is beautiful and I find the energy very quiet. At this elevation we are probably above a lot of the thought form activity in the city. Have you noticed that thought forms can easily be felt? When I am in a more densely populated area, it is as if every person's mind is broadcasting non-stop; I feel bombarded with the mind babble!"

"I'm sure you're right." I mused. "It does seem amazingly quiet in my mental body. In crowded places I often experience an unpleasant hum of noise created by the constant chatter making it challenging to feel peaceful.

After a moment I said, "I keep waiting for the clear messages we received from our Spirit indicating that we are to move here to somehow change. So far the message that this is our place is just getting stronger."

Our food arrived and we sat in comfortable silence enjoying the taste and texture of each bite. Qua was right, the atmosphere felt very peaceful and still.

Leaving the restaurant we became aware that night hit hard and fast in the Colorado Mountains. It felt like the temperature had dipped at least ten degrees under a dazzling night sky. At this elevation and with the lack of humidity, the stars were amazingly bright even with the full moon. We were transfixed by the site of Pikes Peak rising dramatically in the distance illuminated by the moon and the sparkling stars overhead.

Although we had only spent a little over an hour in Woodland Park, we were now certain that this was the place we were destined to find.

"Do you think we are supposed to continue our trip through New Mexico and back through California or just head back the way we came?" Qua asked.

"I feel we are to continue on our original path." I said quietly

"Then let's get back on the road and head south before stopping tonight."

As we drove back down the mountain toward Colorado Springs, I contemplated our shared practice of following our inner voice (Spirit) rather than the dictates of the outer world.

Qua and I share, individually and together, an inner landscape that says following your Spirit without hesitation is the only choice to make. If the world is to be re-born into a higher spiritual reality, it is necessary that we serve our inner authority and knowing. When people get busy trying to please others or follow the rules established by outer authority, they lose themselves to outside needs and demands, becoming deaf to their own inner voice.

In spiritual communities it is common for people to give themselves up to outside authority in the form of ministers, teachers or gurus. This is just another form of following something on the 'outside' versus the 'inside' where Spirit resides.

To us it is obvious that even if people set themselves up in a context of student and teacher, all they can ever experience are their own insights about the teacher's insights. If someone states something and it resonates as true within you, then it is your truth. No two people will translate the same information in exactly the same way. As we fill ourselves with more divine truth through

life experiences and insights, our personal vibration increases and we impact
everything in the Universe.

As we continued our journey south, my mind began to worry. What will
I do about my horses? What about the church group. We don't know enough
about basic considerations such as rental costs. Looking over I noticed that
Qua seemed very deep in thought with a small frown on his face.

"What are you thinking about?" I asked

"I'm wondering how we are going to make this move. It will be very
expensive. Once we get here, I doubt there are any high tech companies
where I could get a job if we got in trouble financially."

"My mind was going down the same vein! I sure hope our councils have
taken all of this into consideration and are preparing the way for us!" I
exclaimed.

Suddenly we heard uproarious laughter in our merged mind with the
clear thought, "You have enough money to get here—what more is needed?"
followed by more cosmic delight.

As the laughter danced and sparkled in the air, I looked over at Qua.
Meeting his eyes I began to laugh so hard and so deep that tears rolled down
my cheeks and I was forced to clutch my ribs.

After the waves of humor subsided, Qua muttered, "I guess we're not
going to get any information beyond the fact that Woodland Park is to be our
new home. We'll discover why when it all plays out. As usual, Spirit does not
give us a view of the future, only a knowing of the present moment. The future
is in the mystery; beyond understanding by the mind.

I nodded in agreement. "Life is very confusing, scary and difficult for
many people in this reality because they are attempting to figure it all out and
control the outcome. In my knowing, we are actors on a stage in a play that has

darkness and light and is forever reforming itself. The only choice we have is to move with the flow or resist it. One choice brings peace and acceptance; the other brings pain and suffering. The only way to find joy and purpose in all of it is to allow ourselves to be guided through the maze by an inner voice or higher Self/Spirit. The thinking mind is not designed to maneuver the pitfalls. It can only lead us into what it knows—repeating the past."

With Qua, I realized that we were in complete understanding and spoke the same language. Subtle vibrations of peace, love and lightness flowed through the space around us. In the presence of this very special Soul inhabiting a human form, I knew I had found my spiritual partner and that together we would accomplish our unified soul's mission to assist in the birth of a new consciousness, A New World.

Epilogue

We completed our trip over the next week, stopping in Santa Fe, New Mexico and on to Sedona, Arizona to visit with KemDara and Drakar, our Earth Mission friends.

The trip through California felt especially poignant. California was not a place for us to settle, yet our bodies recognized it as having been an important part of our life journey. Seldom had we experienced such beauty. After a rainy spring, there were massive displays of wildflowers and lushly green grasses waving in the wind across the hills and valleys. We were captivated by the little blue star flowers, yellow buttercups, and California Poppies among the tall, lacy spears of white wildflowers.

We drove up the coastal highway, stopping to rent a cabin in Big Sur for a couple of days. It was revitalizing to be in our own orbit where everything flowed with ease and grace. We could feel ourselves merging with a larger purpose, a bigger picture that was yet to be fully revealed.

Arriving back in Chehalis after our ten day trip with all of its amazing experiences, I felt like I was walking into a community that was from a life separate from me. It was as if I had read a book or watched a movie with a vivid plot and was coming out of the experience with wisps of energy still travelling through my awareness.

Over the next few weeks we methodically completed arrangements to move—packing, giving notice to my landlord, getting rid of massive amounts of stuff, arranging for movers and finding a home for the animals.

Juelle and Donovan organized a good-bye party in our honor. It allowed some level of completion with those who attended. However there were others in the spiritual community still too wrapped up in their perceived drama and judgments to participate.

In truth, what people think of us has everything to do with the person doing the thinking. Whether a person criticizes or idolizes another, they are only reflecting their own consciousness onto an outside form. If a person sees themselves as a small human being rather than a spiritual essence, they will constantly compare themselves to others and attempt to control the outside world in order to survive and uphold a personal identity. Where true peace and power resides is in each person's inner world, that part of us that is everlasting and never changing, waiting to be acknowledged and therefore awakened into full expression.

In less than a month, we were on our way to Colorado without a clue where we were going to live, other than in Woodland Park, or why we were being sent to this community. It was the end of one phase of the story and the beginning of a grand new adventure—as is always true in this spiritual quest we call life.

Blessings on your journey!
Vishara and Qua

Questions and Answers

From the Silence Beyond Time
"The Joining"

The following is a transcript of a question and answer session held with a group who recently read the manuscript of this book. All answers represent our attempt to express multidimensional realities in the English language.

Why did you write this book?

We wrote the book because our Spirits instructed us to do so. I also believe the energy of the earth is now ready for this information; however, we did not analyze the reasons before deciding to begin writing the book. The highest value available for readers of "The Joining" is stimulation to assist in the awakening to their True Identity.

The thought of writing a book seemed like a daunting task. It took years to get started in earnest. One morning I awoke and knew it was time. I began writing and felt stimulated to send the first chapters to Joanne Atwood, a published author and Spiritual Sister, who became very enthusiastic. She has been my inspiration and has both embodied and co-written sections of *"The Joining"*. When it is in Divine Timing to act upon an idea, Spirit provides an abundance of energy to accomplish the task. The Universe rearranges Itself to accommodate your success.

Will you explain more about the 'walk-in' experience?

Everyone walked in when they were born. The soul inhabits a body near the time of birth and is the frequency that animates and provides life force. The human body is only a form with a beginning, middle and end.

The difference between the way in which Qua and I entered into adult bodies and that of being born into it is merely timing. As we arrived, the original souls, Danielle and Tony, left before the body died.

A major advantage of the walk-in experience is the fact that you are entering a mature body. Therefore, you have all your facilities; you can attempt to speak about what you experienced whereas a baby cannot.

Why did the walk-in happen? Why not just come in at birth?

The phenomenon of the walk-in occurrence isn't really important. For whatever reason it describes our spiritual adventure; other people have different kinds of awakening experiences. We aren't representing walk-ins as being a better occurrence than other types of spontaneous enlightenment, or, the commonly known, very gradual growth to awakening.

We can only guess as to why it happened. We have attempted to put into words our experience because people are less familiar with the phenomena and want to better understand it. The original souls in these bodies made an agreement with their soul family and partners (Qua and Vishara, among others) prior to their birth on earth.

When you come into a body later in its lifespan, the pain and suffering of life's journeys are not experienced so intensely. It is easy for Qua and I to go to an elevated level in consciousness where it is not necessary to deal as directly with all the veils that were put into place by Danielle and Tony. Not that we do not feel them, they are still being accessed in the cells of these bodies. It is just that the distortions do not make sense to us and, therefore are experienced as less real.

Even more important is the Divine Plan and its specific timing for this realm. Qua and I were pre-destined to come onto the planet with these frequencies to assist in a new possibility being born. The smaller body of an infant or child would not be compatible with our energies.

The problem with sharing yourself as a walk-in, or a channel, is that it is a label and, therefore, very limiting. People try to put you in a mental place that has all kinds of preconceived ideas and expectations—many of which have nothing to do with the Truth. Our journey took us down these pathways because it was the highest possibility for our particular mission.

I can see how it would make it easier to enter into a body of an adult, then you can hit the ground running. I'm wondering what is in it for the original inhabitants, Danielle and Tony, who were born into your bodies?

They were transmuting energy their entire lifetime. They were evolving spiritually and living their journey. What's in it for anyone who lives and dies? They left the body to go to their next expression which is not a bad thing—it's just the next thing for them. In truth, it's a very good thing!

One of the functions of the first inhabitant is to clear the way and get the body into a situation that is conducive to allowing the new soul to enter. It is their destiny to do that. It was a soul to soul contract before birth.

As walk-ins, Qua and I came in with recent memories of our other-dimensional experiences of Home. We moved from a much more expanded place into the constraints of this earthly reality and attempted to figure it all out.

Souls who have lived a life-time in a body are often trying to get out of this consciousness into higher frequency realities. This is especially true for beings in the human potential movement. We are on the opposite end of the same journey. We arrived into bodies still in conscious communication with our spiritual councils. Our challenge was to get into these denser forms.

Why would you want to become denser to get into a body?

Just like a newborn baby, a walk-in is not very functional. Even though our bodies were fully developed, we were not familiar with how to behave, or the rules of engagement. Our second book will include the story of the things we needed to learn. For example, where we come from there is absolutely no attachment to things; no ownership, no comparisons or judgments of others. It is quite different here.

Completing our mission required being in bodies. This human reality asked everything of us in order to put up enough veils to get fully integrated. Of course that is true of most people—usually that learning is in early childhood. We spent years in an attempt to become fully engaged in this reality.

Note: If you want more detailed information about walk-ins, visit our web site where we have a list of recommended books and sites including one that addresses the walk-in phenomena in detail. *www.awake2oneness.com*

So, our journey is to start out clear, learn how to be dense and then reverse out of it back to more clarity?

That's right. We call it the spiritualization of matter. It is easier to have a primary identity as a vast spiritual being when you are a walk-in. You know that the human identity is temporary because the body in which you reside will die.

When you are more spiritually awake, more is asked of you in support of evolution. For example Jesus came into a lifetime remembering his Spiritual identity and the true identity of all people. He had the miraculous capacity to hold the fear of the world in his human expression and shine the Light of Truth/God onto those distortions. Jesus knew Himself to be a Spiritual Being, inhabiting a human body, on a mission to transmute energies into Love for the whole matrix on this planet. That is what is meant when it is said that through Jesus, sins are forgiven.

Qua, is this your first lifetime in this reality?

Yes, my experience is that I don't have a past life on this planet. I have some faint recollections of some other home planet, on another level. I don't have any information about what those lifetimes were like; only that my home planet is not Earth.

Qua, the clothes you were wearing throughout the book seemed to be very important.

Yes, the clothes carried a frequency that assisted in keeping me in touch with my councils and supporting the vibrational shift in preparation for the walk-in experience. As we moved more deeply into the world, I stopped wearing the clothing and now dress appropriately for my current assignment.

What is meant by 'following your Spirit'?

Following your Spirit refers to being present and listening to that still, small impulse inside. The next step is acting on that, rather than on thoughts and considerations that the mind may introduce. Many people find it easiest to access that impulse through body sensations; bypassing the constant chatter of the mind.

It is important to know that the thinking mind and the pain body (fear) are only dealing with the past and future possibilities based on what they think they know. Nothing new is created. The mind and pain body merely repeat what has already been. The mind scans the past and begins analyzing trying to figure out how to avoid repeating pain, or, how to get, or hold onto, something it likes. Most people stay in the same loop lifetime after lifetime until it is too painful to continue.

Moving into a new reality requires following your Spirit; that quick knowing deep inside that immediately responds with direction for the next moment. Immediately after your Spirit communicates, the mind will react with reasons to agree or disagree. Qua and I follow that first impulse to the best of our ability moment to moment. The future is left in the mystery.

For example, Qua left Silicon Valley and his career. He didn't know where it would take him; he had no destination in mind. The same was true when he and I got together. Being assigned to another person for a joint spiritual mission was a complete surprise for both of us.

What makes things seem hard and difficult is the mind's attempts to figure everything out. The mind tries to control the future, or identify with past experiences and struggles. When you live only in present time, life is filled with ease and grace. From our true, expanded reality, nothing is hard; it just is what it is in that moment.

I'm concerned that people reading "The Joining" will think they need to find a spiritual partner, or spouse, even if it means walking away from everything and everyone as you and Qua did. I don't think that is meant for everyone. Are we intended to have a partner, or are some of us meant to be single?

We are clear that finding a spiritual partner isn't the highest and best possibility in everyone's life. It just happened to be our destiny. The reason we were able to walk away from friends, family and our work was because we value the call of our inner knowing (Spirit) over that of the mind, other people's opinions, or perceived needs being projected on us. In our case, the highest expression for our mission was to be together.

One of the things valued in this reality is to have a mate or partner. The very act of thinking you "need" something is counter-productive to getting it. You already *are* everything; your True Self needs nothing.

The world renowned spiritual teacher, Eckhart Tolle and many others, teach acceptance of what is. If you are resisting what is happening in this moment, then you're fighting against reality. If you experience difficulty accepting something; then just accept that you are having difficulty and go on.

If being with a life partner is the highest spiritual expression for you, then one will come into your life. If not, it is because you are best served in some other way.

Did the fact that you are walk-ins make it possible to ignore the pull of others as you followed your Spiritual Direction?

The previous inhabitants, Danielle and Tony, were also surrendered to being directed by Spirit. Had they been directed to blend their lives with each other—even without being walk-ins—they would have followed that calling wherever it took them. It does not require a certain spiritual experience. It was a matter of what we valued, which was to follow our Spirit above everything and everyone else.

Aren't you concerned about people trying to emulate you and therefore experiencing tremendous pain by walking away from everything just because something inside asks them to leave what they have now?

It seems evident that there is also tremendous pain in staying where you aren't meant to be. It's sometimes a slower pain; it is the pain of giving yourself into the hands of the needs of others or, into your own fear. We are ALL Spiritual Beings living in a human body whether we recognize, or value, that Truth or not.

Qua and I do not make decisions or take action based on pain, obligation or fear. If those emotions are accessing us, we start moving energy to the Light and wait until our Spiritual impulses are clear once more. We would never have been together, or moved to Woodland Park, if we had been listening to the voice in our heads. To our thinking mind both of those choices were crazy.

I have a question about channeling. Aren't you concerned that a negative energy might come through you?

In the beginning I certainly had that concern. However, my inner wisdom assured me that the only way a lower frequency being (negative energy) could come through is on an energy wave of fear. Low frequency beings cannot travel in when you fill your heart with Love and Truth because like frequencies attract like frequencies.

Vishara, how do you recognize it when your councils or channeled entities are communicating?

Zantron and the rest of my council, to a large extent, are integrated into my inner life and give me downloads of information quite often. It comes to me without thought or analysis. I just suddenly completely know about something or someone.

Qua what do you see when your council speaks to you? Can you see them physically?

Not any longer. They used to be quite vivid. Now I only sense them. When I first came in I wasn't very far into this body so my consciousness was closer to my council and other subtle realities. Now it is like a telepathic conversation. I do know that one of their functions is to network and connect people and things around the planet.

What are you hoping people will get out of reading "The Joining"*?*

We want the book to give readers the vicarious experience of living a life primarily indentifying yourself as a Spiritual Being. The new world that is awakening in consciousness, and it is occurring now, will be lived in ways demonstrated in "The Joining". People who are on the leading edge of this great new era will be attracted to this book. "The Joining" is intended to wake up parts of Spiritual Consciousness that may be just under the surface. It will not matter if a person has been pursuing a spiritual path or not; if the time is right, it will stimulate a new level of awareness.

This new elevated reality is based on energy and spiritual frequency—there is an expanded level of commitment, support and courage available to all who surrender to co-creating their mission on Earth.

It is not necessary to have been seekers for many years; taking every spiritual workshop available and/or reading book after book. Everyone is the same at the core. We are only pretending to be a human with a specific personality and belief system. Everyone has the potential to wake up in any moment. When the time is right all will join together in the new world.

More questions or comments?

Visit our web site: www.awake2oneness.com

About the Authors

Vishara and Qua Veda offer stimulation that can point you toward your True Identity—the Oneness—the Absolute expressing Itself into multiple dimensions of relative existence.

This is the spiritualization of matter and the awakening of a new world in consciousness!

Qua and Vishara Veda live on a ranch in western Oregon with their five Andalusian horses and four cats.

Joanne Atwood also lives in Oregon and can be contacted through Twitter, Facebook or www.awake2oneness. She has been invaluable in the process of completing this book.

For more information:
www.awake2oneness.com
"Join our blog and/or sign up for Free Newsletter"

- Spiritual perspectives
- Audio and video presentations
- Speaking engagements, Book Signing/Readings
- Newsletters and inspirational messages emailed to you
- Retreats
- Online classes
- Recommendations of products, services and books available through others
- Updates on our offerings and products

LaVergne, TN USA
23 October 2009
161727LV00005B/6/P